BUILDING YOUR OWN
Robots

by Gordon McComb

WILEY

BUILDING YOUR OWN ROBOTS

Published by
John Wiley & Sons, Inc.
111 River Street
Hoboken, NJ 07030-5774

www.wiley.com

Copyright © 2016 by John Wiley & Sons, Inc., Hoboken, NJ

Published simultaneously in Canada

For general information on our other products and services, please contact our Customer Care Department within the U.S. at 877-762-2974, outside the U.S. at 317-572-3993, or fax 317-572-4002. For technical support, please visit https://hub.wiley.com/community/support/dummies.

Wiley publishes in a variety of print and electronic formats and by print-on-demand. Some material included with standard print versions of this book may not be included in e-books or in print-on-demand. If this book refers to media such as a CD or DVD that is not included in the version you purchased, you may download this material at http://booksupport.wiley.com. For more information about Wiley products, visit www.wiley.com.

Library of Congress Control Number: 2016947914

ISBN: 978-1-119-30243-8 (pbk); 978-1-119-30245-2 (ebk); 978-1-119-30244-5 (ebk)

Manufactured in the United States of America

10 9 8 7 6 5 4 3 2 1

CONTENTS

PROJECT 2: BUILD A ROBOT FROM A TOY CAR   29

PROJECT 3: BUILD A MOUSEBOT   53

PROJECT 4: HACK A RADIO-CONTROLLED TOY 78

AUTHOR NOTES 114

GLOSSARY 118

INTRODUCTION GET STARTED WITH ROBOT-BUILDING

WELCOME TO THE WORLD OF ROBOT-BUILDING! When I was a kid I saw a scary movie about robots. But instead of being afraid, it made me want to build my own "mechanical man."

My very first robot wasn't a robot at all — it was just a tin can with wires sticking out the top. But it started me on a lifelong journey of building stuff that moved and blinked . . . some of my robots have even walked and talked.

ABOUT THIS BOOK

Robot building isn't just one skill, it's a whole lot of them.

In order to build a robot, you have to learn how to use tools, craft new things out of existing parts or raw materials, apply basic concepts of electricity to motors and switches, plus much more.

Building Your Own Robots helps teach you these and other core concepts, while showing you how to construct four different fun and interesting robots. Each of the four projects in this book is designed to be inexpensive, and they each require no more than two hours of building time. Special tools aren't needed.

You'll discover things like:

» Understanding the important parts of a robot

» Making robots from discarded toys and common household materials

» How to use small motors to make your robot creations *m-o-v-e*

» Using batteries to power your robot

Everything is designed for kids. None of the building plans require using sharp or dangerous tools. (Still, be sure to read and follow all the safety guidelines provided!)

What this book isn't about: Sorry, this book won't teach you how to build your own R2-D2 or C-3PO. Those kinds of robots are far more complicated than what can be explained here.

But when you're done with this book, and you want to discover more, don't stop! See "Finding the Stuff to Build Your Robots," at the back of this book, for a list of resources for continuing your robot-building education.

BASIC TOOLS AND SUPPLIES

Here's what you need to do the projects in this book:

» Some common household tools, including scissors, a small screwdriver, and a pair of needle nosed pliers. Don't worry — each project details the specific tools you need to complete the robot.

» A low temperature hot glue gun and a spool of black electrical tape.

» Some discarded toothbrushes, toys, and other household items, raided for their parts. If you don't already have these hiding somewhere in your closet, you can find them easily enough at garage sales and resale stores. They also are cheap to buy new.

» Insulated wire — when the time comes, I'll tell you exactly what kind.

» Foam board (the stuff you make school projects with) or thick cardboard cut from a shipping box.

» Small toy hobby motors. Get these from junk stuff, or buy new. They're cheap.

» Quarter-inch (outside diameter) clear aquarium tubing, for making tiny tires. Get it at pet-supply stores and most home improvement outlets.

ABOUT YOU

Any book with projects has to make a few assumptions about the folks who read them. To get the most out of this book, my assumption is that you have:

» Some basic familiarity with using simple tools — screwdrivers, scissors, and hot melt glue guns for crafting.

» Some familiarity with making simple things out of adhesive tape, glue, thick cardboard, and foam boards. You don't need to be an expert; this book will help you improve your skills.

» Patience. This is this most important skill you need to successfully — and happily! — build your own robots. Go slowly, and enjoy the experience. Don't rush!

FOR PARENTS

The projects in *Building Your Own Robots* are designed so that most children 7 and older can reproduce them without significant parental supervision.

All four projects include "Going Further" sections that cover intermediate topics found online. For some of these, parental guidance is highly recommended.

The steps in these "Going Further" sections are completely optional and are not part of the basic project. Instead, use them as "extra credit" for enjoying the exploration of science and technology with your child or student.

ABOUT THE ICONS

You'll encounter a few picture icons as you read through the projects in this book. The icons point out different things:

Discover great ideas and time-saving shortcuts with the Tip icon.

Proceed with caution! This icon warns you of potential mistakes that could result in project failure, lost time, or even damage to your robot.

The Remember icon reminds you of great concepts you've encountered before and should keep in mind while building.

Okay, then. Let's get started!

PROJECT 1 MAKE A BRUSHBOT, FAST AND EASY!

NOT ALL ROBOTS ROLL ON WHEELS OR WALK ON LEGS. Some of them look like centipedes and slither on the ground. Others fly in the air on their own. And a few even shake and shimmy across the floor on hundreds of tiny tentacles.

Wait . . . shake? Shimmy? *Tiny tentacles*? You bet! Introducing the *brushbot*, a battery operated robotic creature that's both super-fun and easy to build.

The brushbot isn't a new idea, and you may even have seen one in action in a YouTube video. But not all brushbots are alike. The plans I detail in this project take less than 15 minutes to complete, require no soldering, and cost less than a hamburger lunch.

Robot building doesn't get much easier than this!

UNDERSTANDING WHAT MAKES A ROBOT

To understand how to make your own robot, you first need to know the basic parts that go into all robots.

Sensors *Manipulation*

Brains *Sound*

Movement *Power*

Robots are created out of different *subsystems*. These include *power*, *brains*, *sensors*, and *movement*. The subsystems work together to create the finished robot. Not every robot has all subsystems. Some specialty robots lack one or more of these subsystems or have additional ones not shown here. That's okay . . . they're still robots.

For example, many combat robots, like those in the TV show *Robot Wars*, are operated by a human via remote control. The robot may not have an onboard brain. Other robots may not have any parts that move. Instead, they might interact with humans using a video camera and computer display.

The brushbot project contains only a few of the subsystems found in robots — namely, just power and movement. Additional robot subsystems are shown in other projects in this book.

BUILDING YOUR FIRST ROBOT: MAKE A BRUSHBOT "WALKING" ROBOT

The brushbot consists of just a few parts: A vibrating "engine," a battery to power the engine, and a small brush that provides hundreds of teeny, wobbly "legs."

Electrical terminals for wiring to battery

Motor   *Off-balance weight*

The *vibrating engine* is just a fancy term for a toy motor that has an off-centered weight attached to its shaft. The weight is on crooked, so when the motor turns, the imbalance causes everything to shake. The motor vibrates. When it's attached to a robot, the vibration literally makes the bot bounce up and down.

The vibrating motor on a brushbot is attached to a small brush. The brush serves as a *low-friction* surface that allows the brushbot to move. *Friction* is the force that is created between two touching objects. Friction can be high or low.

» **High friction** causes objects to stick together. Gym shoes on an asphalt driveway is an example of high friction.

» **Low friction** causes objects to slip and slide. Think stuff like ice and ice skates.

The ends of brush bristles are teeny-tiny small. That smallness equates to very low friction between the bristles and the smooth surface of a floor or table. Thanks to the low friction from the bristles, the brushbot is free to vibrate and move as it pleases.

FOR VIBRATING MOTORS: HACK YOUR TOOTHBRUSH

So now you know your brushbot needs a couple of principal ingredients. Let's start with the vibrating motor.

Although you could probably make a vibrating motor from scratch, it's a heck of a lot easier to just rob one that's already made. But where do you find such a thing?

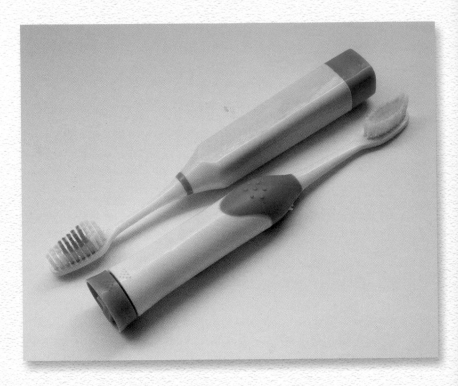

One of the best (and cheapest) sources is a *battery-operated* electric toothbrush. Nowadays, these things are disposable — use it for a month or two, and when it gets all funky, buy a new one. The electric toothbrushes I used in my prototypes each cost a dollar and were found at — you guessed it — the dollar store.

Note the phrase battery-operated! *To build a brushbot, your toothbrush must run off batteries — **not** plug into the wall. Don't ever try to hack a toothbrush that's powered by an electrical outlet. Not only would such a toothbrush simply not work in this project, but if you were to plug it into a socket, it could also give you a nasty and potentially fatal electric shock!*

WHAT ABOUT OLD VIBRATOR MOTORS FROM JUNKED CELL PHONES?

Some of the brushbot plans found on the Internet use a teeny vibrator motor from a discarded cell phone. These are okay, but in my experience, they aren't as easy to use. First, you have to take the cell phone completely apart, and these days most phones are designed to make this as difficult as possible.

Second, a phone vibrator motor is quite small, and it can be hard (sometimes impossible) to surgically remove one without ruining it.

USE JUST THE RIGHT BRISTLE BRUSH

To make a speedy brushbot, you need the right kind of brush. The ideal brush for your brushbot measures no more than about 2" by 3". A scrub brush for cleaning vegetables is one good choice. Try to find one that's flat on the back.

Be sure your brush

» **Is lightweight.** The heavier the brush, the harder your brushbot must work to move.

» **Uses stiff bristles.** Stay away from brushes with heavy bristles, or have bristles with rubber tips. These things increase friction.

» **Doesn't have a plethora of bristles.** If it does, you can give it a trim around the edges, using a pair of scissors.

When trimming bristles, be sure to wear goggles or other eye protection to keep the bits and pieces from flying into your eyes.

MATERIALS YOU NEED

There are two versions of brushbot — simple and "open guts":

» The **simple** version requires almost no construction. You use the electric toothbrush practically as it comes out of its packaging.

» In the **open guts** version, you remove the vibrator motor and battery compartment from the toothbrush handle.

To complete either version of the project, you need these materials:

rubber band
(see text)

battery

small scrub brush

battery-operated
toothbrush

electrical tape

Both versions

1 Battery-operated electric toothbrush (see text and "Finding the Stuff to Build Your Robots," at the back of this book)

1 AA alkaline or heavy-duty flashlight battery (may already come with toothbrush)

1 Small vegetable or scrubbing brush (see text)

Open guts version only

1 Roll of electrical tape

1 Medium-size rubber band

TOOLS YOU NEED

To complete this project, you need these tools:

hot melt glue gun, with glue stick (low temp ok)

scissors (careful-sharp!)

needle nosed pliers with side cutter

see text if you'll need these tools

safety goggles

nail

hobby saw

Both versions

Hot melt glue gun, and glue stick

Open guts version only

Scissors

Small needle nosed pliers

If you have to cut off the top of the toothbrush to get to the motor, you might also need: small craft saw, protective eyewear, nail

With all the tools and materials in hand, it's time to build!

MAKING THE BRUSHBOT – SIMPLE VERSION

Depending on the battery-operated toothbrush you use, the simple version of the brushbot requires virtually no physical building — just remove the brushing part of the toothbrush, glue the toothbrush handle to the top of your veggie or scrubbing brush, and let 'er rip!

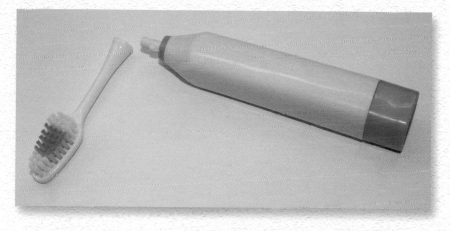

1 **On many battery-operated electric toothbrushes, the toothbrush head — the part you actually brush your teeth with — is removable. Just turn the brush to unlock it from the handle. (If the brush head on your electric toothbrush is permanently attached, see the nearby sidebar, "So, Your Electric Toothbrush Doesn't Use Removable Brush Heads.")**

2 **Remove the battery cover and insert a battery. Most battery-operated electric toothbrushes use one AA-size battery cell.**

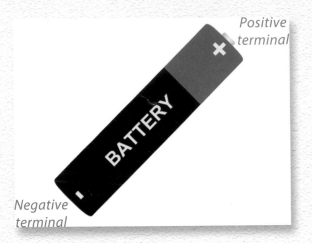

Positive terminal

Negative terminal

TIP

Observe the proper polarity of the battery — that is, which end is + (positive), and which end is – (negative). Batteries use the symbols + and – to denote polarity. On most toothbrushes, the battery goes in – (negative) end first.

3 **Momentarily flip the power switch on to test operation. The motor inside the toothbrush handle should hum, and you should feel the vibration.**

4 **Apply several blobs of glue from the hot melt glue gun to the bottom of the toothbrush handle. One blob near each end and one in the middle should be enough.**

5 **Swiftly but carefully stick the handle squarely to the back of the scrub brush. Hold it there for a few seconds until the glue has cooled.**

6 **Use the hot melt gun to apply a bead of glue down the edges of the handle. Let cool completely.**

Your brushbot is now complete! Put it on the ground — polished kitchen tile is best — and switch it on. The robot should slowly boogie across the floor. Push it to make it move in different directions.

Your brushbot will work on most smooth, flat surfaces. Forget carpet; there's too much friction. Tabletops, kitchen and bathroom counters, and hardwood floors are your best bet.

Brushbots make great cat toys! But use care when introducing your cat — or any other animal — to your robots. Some cats are scared of the sounds and abrupt motions of a robot in action. Don't hold your kitteh while powering up your new robot, or you could get badly scratched. Let Fluffy meet and greet your brushbot on her own terms.

SO, YOUR ELECTRIC TOOTHBRUSH DOESN'T USE REMOVABLE BRUSH HEADS

It's a slam-dunk if your electric toothbrush has a removable brush head. Just twist off the head, and you're all set. But what happens if the head is permanently attached to the toothbrush handle?

You can still use the toothbrush, but you'll need to do a little bit of surgery to remove the head. It involves cutting with a hobby saw.

Before following these steps, be sure the toothbrush is working by inserting a battery and switching it on.

Ask a parent, teacher, or other adult for permission before using a hobby saw. Although these saws are safe when handled properly, you should still exercise care to avoid cuts or scratches.

Wear goggles or other eye protection when cutting. *This keeps the bits of plastic cut from the toothbrush from getting into your eyes.*

1 Clear off your table, and use a pad of writing paper to make a work area.

2 Hold the toothbrush handle in one hand, and in the other, use the saw to cut off the *very top* portion of the brush head. Cut very slowly and very carefully!

3 When you've cut about two-thirds of the way through, stop sawing, and use gentle finger pressure to snap the head off the body of the toothbrush.

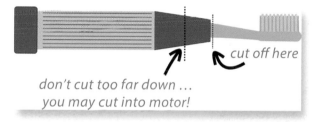

cut off here

*don't cut too far down …
you may cut into motor!*

4 When the cutting is complete, wipe away any plastic bits that remain.

MAKING THE BRUSHBOT – OPEN GUTS VERSION

You might want to give a more techno look to your brushbot by exposing the working parts. The open guts version is much the same as the simplified version, except that you remove the motor and battery compartment from the toothbrush handle.

REMEMBER

Test the toothbrush first before hacking. Do this by inserting a fresh battery into the handle and switching the toothbrush on. Be sure to observe the direction of the battery in the toothbrush. On many toothbrushes, the – (negative) end of the battery goes in first.

REMOVE THE BATTERY COMPARTMENT AND MOTOR FROM THE TOOTHBRUSH

Time now to get the guts of your toothbrush out into the open:

1 **Remove the battery cover from the bottom of the toothbrush handle. If there's a battery inside, take it out and set it aside.**

2 **Look into the brush handle: You should see a plastic battery compartment nestled inside. With just your finger, try to *gently* pull the plastic compartment out of the toothbrush handle.**

Don't yank too hard or you may pull the battery compartment away from the motor. You might be able to loosen things up by rapping the bottom of the toothbrush handle against the tabletop.

Either of two things might now happen:

Pull out gently!

» The battery compartment comes free, and with it, the vibrating motor, all in one piece. Yippee!

» The compartment is stuck in the toothbrush handle and exerting more force could wreck things. If that's the case, see the next series of steps.

ONLY IF NEEDED: CUT OFF THE BRUSH HEAD

If the battery compartment and motor are lodged in tight, you'll need to cut off the brush head so you can push out the motor from the top. You'll use a craft (or hobby) saw for this.

See the sidebar, "So, Your Electric Toothbrush Doesn't Use Removable Brush Heads," for basic info on cutting up your toothbrush.

Ask a parent, teacher, or other adult for permission before using cutting tools. Though safe when handled properly, these tools still require care to avoid cuts or scratches.

Wear goggles or other eye protection when cutting.

1 Clear off your table, and use a pad of writing paper to make a work area.

2 If your toothbrush uses a removable brush head, take it off from the brush handle.

3 Hold the handle of the toothbrush in one hand and hold the saw in your other. Cut off the top portion of the toothbrush handle. Cut slowly and carefully.

4 After cutting, look down the top of the toothbrush; you should see the motor inside. Use a small nail to push the motor out the bottom.

Be careful to cut just from the top of the toothbrush handle. Otherwise you may saw into the motor shaft, which could wreck both the saw and the motor.

TAPE THE BATTERY COMPARTMENT TO THE MOTOR

If your toothbrush is like the millions of others out there, the battery compartment is electrically connected to the motor using simple pieces of metal. There's nothing to hold the battery compartment and motor together, so you have to add some tape to keep things from coming apart:

1 **Cut a piece of electrical tape to about 5" in length.**

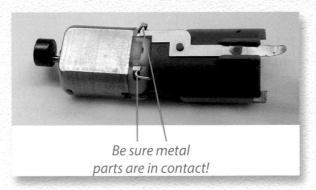

Be sure metal parts are in contact!

2 **Be sure both metal contacts are still touching the two terminals on the motor. If they're not touching, your brushbot won't work.**

If the contacts get separated from the motor terminals, use a pair of needle nosed pliers to gently work things back into position. The terminals are fragile and can be easily broken off, so be careful!

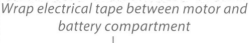

Wrap electrical tape between motor and battery compartment

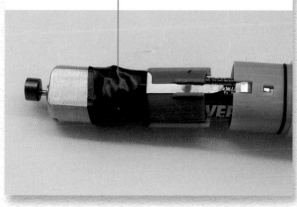

3 Apply the electrical tape to hold the battery compartment and motor together.

TEST THE MOTOR

As you build any robot, it's always good to test it at various times to make sure things still work as expected. Now is a good time to test the motor and battery connections of your brushbot:

1 Insert a battery into the battery compartment.

On many electric toothbrushes, the battery is inserted – (negative) end first.

2 Slide the power switch to the On position.

3 Place the battery cover over the end of the battery. Make sure the metal contacts in both the battery compartment and the cover are touching.

Nothing happens? Check these things:

» The battery is inserted the proper way, usually – (negative) end first.

» The metal parts on both the battery compartment and the cover are touching. You may need to physically press them together to make full contact.

4 For now, remove the battery cover and set it and the battery aside.

ATTACH A RUBBER BAND TO HOLD THE BATTERY COVER IN PLACE

The battery cover needs to be held in place using a rubber band:

1 Hook one end of a medium-size rubber band under the motor shaft and draw the band to the bottom of the battery cover.

2 Place the band under the battery compartment cover so that it holds the cover in place.

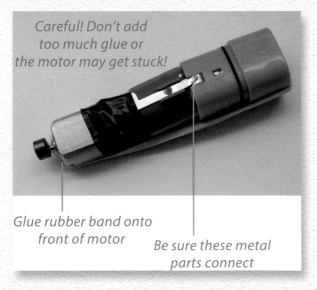

Careful! Don't add too much glue or the motor may get stuck!

Glue rubber band onto front of motor

Be sure these metal parts connect

3 Use a hot melt glue gun to glue on a medium-size rubber band to the very front of the motor. Position it carefully. The rubber band is for keeping the battery cover tightly on the battery compartment.

Apply only a dab of glue and allow it to cool completely before moving or touching the rubber band. If you gob on too much glue, the glue may interfere with the motor, and the brushbot won't work!

4 As needed, apply a 2" length of electrical tape over the metal contacts of the battery compartment and the battery cover to maintain a good connection.

GLUE THE MOTOR TO THE BACK OF THE BRUSH

You're ready to glue the motor onto the top of your brush using a low-temperature hot melt glue gun and glue stick:

1 Orient the motor so that the long metal contact on the battery compartment is facing up.

2 Before adding the glue, "dry fit" the motor and battery compartment over the top of the brush and visualize exactly where you want it to go. For best results, the shaft of the motor should be near the front-center of the brush.

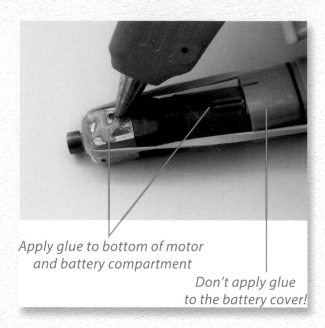

Apply glue to bottom of motor and battery compartment

Don't apply glue to the battery cover!

3 Apply several blobs of glue from the hot melt glue gun to the bottom of the motor and battery compartment.

Don't apply glue to the battery cover. If you do, you won't be able to remove it to change batteries!

4 Swiftly but carefully stick the motor onto the back of the brush. Hold it there for a few seconds until the glue has cooled.

5 Use the hot melt gun to apply a *bead* of more glue around the sides and very front of the motor.

Don't get any glue on the motor's shaft or off-centered weight. If you do, the motor may not turn freely, and your brushbot will not work.

Your brushbot is now ready for play. Put it on a smooth, flat surface, switch it on, and marvel at your genius!

HEY, MY BRUSHBOT DOESN'T GO VERY FAST

The speed your brushbot travels depends on several factors. Here are some reasons your robot might be crawling at a snail's pace and what to do about it:

» **The brush is too large or heavy.** Try to find a smaller and lighter weight brush. The lighter your brushbot, the faster it will go.

» **The brush bristles are too soft.** Try a brush with stiffer bristles.

(continued)

(continued)

> » **The floor isn't smooth enough.** Try a polished hardwood or linoleum floor, or tile or granite kitchen counter.

> » **The battery is worn out.** Replace it with a new one. Use a fresh alkaline or heavy duty battery.

> » **The vibrating motor isn't making solid contact with the top of the brush.** Be sure the motor (or toothbrush handle) is glued on tight.

> » **The motor just isn't powerful enough.** Some battery-operated toothbrushes aren't as powerful as others. Try another brand of inexpensive electric toothbrush, or consider modifying your brushbot to use two batteries instead of just one. See the next section, "Going Further."

GOING FURTHER

There are many ways to build a brushbot — some of them don't even use brushes! Try these ideas, and find more ideas online at www.robotpalace.com/byob/:

Some bonus projects may require help from an adult. See the bonus project plans for details.

» **Scrub brush hard to find?** Try gluing several toothbrush heads together! (Sets of inexpensive regular toothbrushes can be purchased for just a dollar.)

» **Add a second battery.** Replace the one battery with a two-cell battery holder, and operate your brushbot with double the voltage. The result? Your brushbot vibrates more and moves faster!

ROBOTS DON'T ALWAYS HAVE TO BE MADE OF TITANIUM AND STEEL. Plastic will do nicely, thank you very much. Which is great, because plastic is much cheaper and easier to work with!

In this project, you take an ordinary "friction drive" plastic toy car, add a cheapo motor and batteries to it, and turn your homemade creation into a nifty self-propelled robotic vehicle.

This project teaches you crucial construction skills while also demonstrating mechanical and electrical concepts important to building any robot. Plus, it's fun to build, so let's get started!

BUILDING A MOTORIZED ROBOTIC BUGGY

Making a robot from raw materials entails a lot of work. It's easier to use something else as the basis of your robot. Old plastic toy cars and trucks are perfect for this. You might have one in your closet you can use, but if you don't, they're common at garage sales, flea markets, and discount outlets. I bought the one I show in this project for a buck, brand new, at a dollar store.

FIND THE RIGHT TOY CAR

The toy car or truck you want is one that uses a *friction drive* — you give it a push, and a gear mechanism inside the car keeps it zooming across the room. A friction car doesn't have its own motor . . . you'll add that yourself to build your robot buggy.

You can tell if the toy car has a friction drive when you spin the back wheels. Instead of rotating freely, the wheels will resist turning, and you'll hear the gearing mechanics of the friction drive. Let the wheels go, and they'll slowly coast to a stop. That's the friction drive doing its magic.

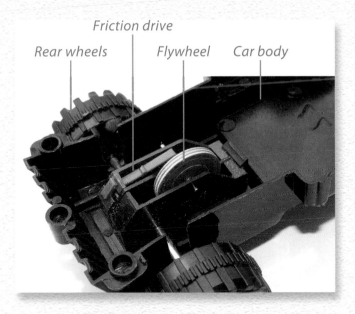

Friction drive

Rear wheels · Flywheel · Car body

You'll probably need to remove the plastic body of the car to expose the friction drive inside. Here's what it should look like.

Notice the thick metal wheel in the middle of the drive. This is the *flywheel*, and it's a necessary part for this project to work. Be sure the car you use has one and that it's out in the open, just like this. In a little bit, I show you how to use a small motor to make this flywheel spin without manually pushing the car.

Your friction toy car needs to look as much like the one in the picture as possible. You might need to take apart a couple of toys to find the right one. Because taking something apart may wreck it, be sure it's a toy you can spare!

If you have trouble snagging a suitable friction drive car for this project, check out the tips and suggestions in "Finding the Stuff to Build Your Robots," at the back of this book.

MATERIALS YOU NEED

To complete this project, you need these materials:

1 Friction car (see the text and "Finding the Stuff to Build Your Robots," at the back of this book)

1 Small 1.5-to-3 volt motor; your buggy won't work well if your motor is made for a higher voltage (see the text and "Finding the Stuff to Build Your Robots")

1 Roll of electrical tape

1 foot 22 gauge stranded wire

2 AAA alkaline or heavy duty flashlight batteries

1" 1/4" diameter (outside dimension) clear tubing; this tubing is about 3/16" inside dimension — aquarium (fish tank) tube is okay, but be sure it's the clear, soft kind

3"x 3" Foam board or thick cardboard

1 Medium-size rubber band

Foam board is the white or colored board you use for school projects. It's made by sandwiching layers of paper on either side of a Styrofoam sheet. Get the stuff that's about 1/4" thick. I recommend using foam board over thick cardboard because it's easier to work with.

TOOLS YOU NEED

To complete this project, you need these tools:

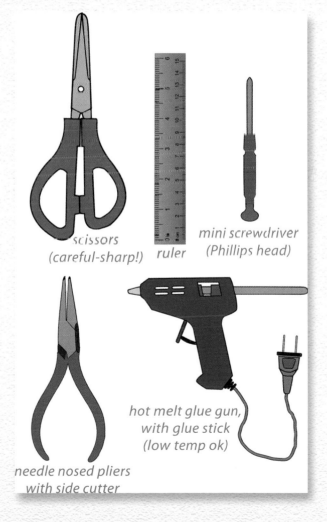

scissors (careful-sharp!) *ruler* *mini screwdriver (Phillips head)*

hot melt glue gun, with glue stick (low temp ok)

needle nosed pliers with side cutter

Small Philips screwdriver

Hot melt glue gun and glue stick

Scissors

Needle nosed pliers with a side cutter, or wire cutters

Ruler, for measuring the lengths of things

WHAT DOES "22 GAUGE STRANDED WIRE" MEAN?

Wire comes in different diameters, referred to as *size*. Wire size is measured in *gauge*. The *lower* the gauge, the *larger* the size — yes, it's true!

All the projects in this book call for 22 gauge wire. It's a common size you can find online, at your local Radio Shack store, and at many home improvement stores. Avoid smaller or larger sizes of wire, which are harder to work with.

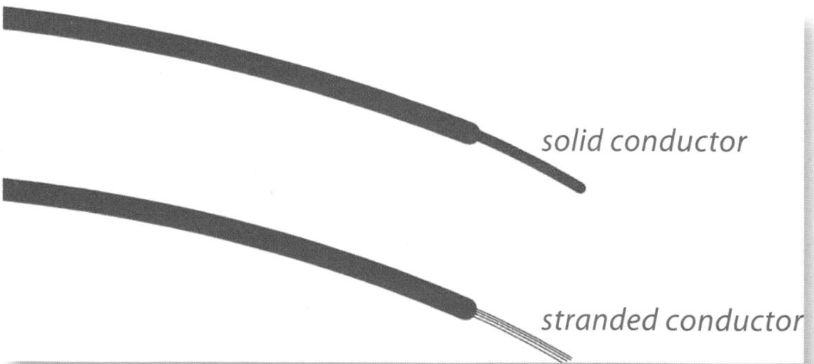

solid conductor

stranded conductor

The *stranded* part means the wire is made of many smaller threads of wire. The other type is called *solid*, and, like its name implies, it's made of just one solid piece of wire. Stranded wire is more bendable, and for this project, it's exactly what you want.

MAKING THE BOT

You're now ready to make your motor-powered car robot.

TAKE THE BODY OFF THE CAR CHASSIS

Start by removing the plastic body from the chassis of the car. You don't need the body for the finished bot.

Most inexpensive toy cars use one or two small screws to attach the body to the chassis. Use a small screwdriver to take out the screws.

Be sure to remove all the screws! Otherwise, the body won't come off easily, and you could break things. Some screws may be hidden in recessed areas, or covered up by paper decals.

There are two common types of screwdrivers: flat and Phillips. Be sure to use the screwdriver type that matches the screw head. Nearly all screws on toy cars are Phillips head.

ADD A RUBBER LAYER TO THE MOTOR SHAFT

The shaft of the motor needs to have a rubber layer added to it. Compare your toy motor with the ones pictured:

Bare shaft

Gear on shaft

If the motor has just a bare metal shaft, you need to thicken it up by wrapping several layers of electrical tape around it and then sticking on a short piece of clear tubing:

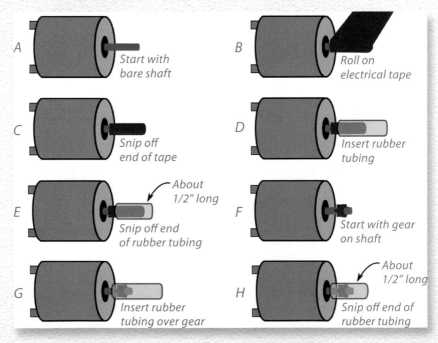

A — Start with bare shaft

B — Roll on electrical tape

C — Snip off end of tape

D — Insert rubber tubing

E — Snip off end of rubber tubing — About 1/2" long

F — Start with gear on shaft

G — Insert rubber tubing over gear

H — Snip off end of rubber tubing — About 1/2" long

1 Cut two pieces of electrical tape to 1-1/2".

2 Carefully apply one of the tape pieces to the shaft. Slowly spin the shaft as the tape rolls onto it. Go slowly and be sure the tape goes on straight!

3 Apply the second piece of tape in the same way.

Rolling the tape onto the motor shaft so that it doesn't leave any crimps or crinkles takes some practice. Don't worry if you make a mistake. Peel off the bad tape and try again with a new piece.

4 Use scissors to snip off the extra tape at the end of the shaft.

5 Cut a piece of aquarium tubing to about 3/4" length.

6 Wet both the tubing and the electrical tape (to make them slippery), and carefully push the tubing over the taped motor shaft.

On the other hand, if there's already a small gear on the motor shaft, odds are you can just fit the aquarium tubing over it:

1 Cut a piece of aquarium tubing to about 3/4" length.

2 Wet both the tubing and the gear, and push the tubing over the motor shaft.

With either of these methods, snip off the end of the tubing so there's about 1/8" extra beyond the motor shaft. The rubber tubing should be about 1/2" long.

WIRE THE MOTOR

Does your motor already have wires already connected to it? Are the wires at least 5" long? If you answered yes to both of these questions, then hurray! You can skip this part. Otherwise, follow the steps below.

For a motor with no wires:

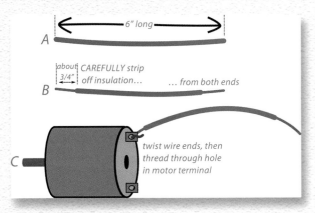

A ⟵ 6" long ⟶

B *about 3/4"* *CAREFULLY strip off insulation…* *… from both ends*

C *twist wire ends, then thread through hole in motor terminal*

1 Use needle nosed pliers with a side cutter (the cutting blade is part of the pliers) to cut two pieces of wire, each to a length of 6".

2 Use the pliers to *carefully* trim off 3/4" of insulation from the ends of both wires. This is tricky work: You want to remove *only* the insulation and not cut the wire. Go slowly. With practice, you'll get the hang of it.

5 Use your fingers to twist the wire strands together in a tight braid.

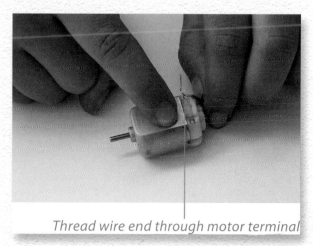

Thread wire end through motor terminal

Twist wire end onto motor terminal

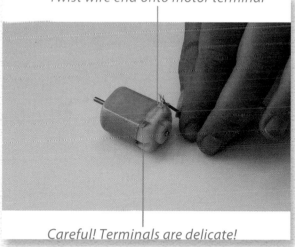

Careful! Terminals are delicate!

4 Take one of the wires, and push it through an eyelet terminal on the motor. Thread it halfway, then twist the wire back around itself, making the wire-to-terminal connection as tight as possible.

5 **Do the same for the other eyelet terminal on the motor.**

For a motor whose wires are already attached but are too short, follow Steps 1 through 3 above. Then

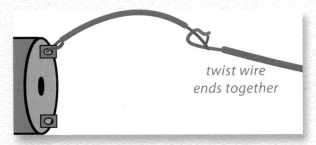

twist wire ends together

4 **Trim 3/4" of insulation from ends of both wires from the motor.**

5 **Twist together the ends of one of the new wires and attach it to a motor wire.**

6 **Repeat for the other motor wire.**

7 **Cut small 1" lengths of electrical tape and wrap them around the exposed connecting parts of the wires.**

Having trouble finding a suitable motor for your robot buggy? Check out "Finding the Stuff to Build Your Robots," at the back of this book, for suggestions on free and low-cost sources for the three-volt toy motor used in this project.

MOUNT THE MOTOR

The motor now needs to be firmly attached to the chassis of the robot buggy. You'll use a hot melt glue gun to stick things together.

All the projects in this book can be assembled using a low temperature hot melt glue gun. These operate at a lower temperature than a standard glue gun, but they still do an excellent job of holding things together.

But — and this is very important — to get the most out of the glue gun, be sure to let it heat up completely before using it. If you don't, the glue won't hold very well, and your project may fall apart. Most glue guns need at least five minutes to reach full temperature.

Even with a low temperature glue gun, you can still get burns from the metal tip of the gun. When applying the glue — which is actually a form of melted plastic — allow at least 20 seconds for it to cool before touching it.

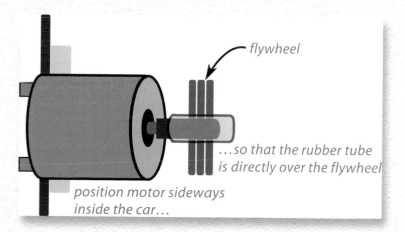

flywheel

...so that the rubber tube is directly over the flywheel

position motor sideways inside the car...

1 Determine where the motor needs to go by placing the shaft (with the rubber tube over it) so that it contacts the flywheel of the friction drive at a right angle.

2 Use that placement to cut pieces of foam core (or thick cardboard) to make one or more mounting strips. For the car I used, I only needed one small piece of foam core, measuring about 1" by 2".

 Unless you use the exact same car, you may need something slightly different. For example, you may find you need to cut several pieces of foam core, and sandwich them together in order to build a bigger shelf for holding the motor at the right spot. Don't be afraid to be creative in making what you have work. Thinking on your own is an important part of robot building!

Glue foam board into car body

3 Use a hot melt glue gun to stick the foam core or cardboard where it needs to go. Let cool (at least a minute) before going to the next step.

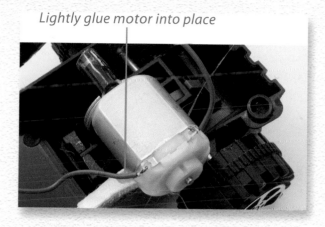

Lightly glue motor into place

4 Position the motor so that the rubber tube sits firmly over the friction wheel.

5 Use your hot melt glue gun to apply a small dab of glue to either side of the motor. Don't put on too much glue — you just want to temporarily *tack* the motor on. This will allow you to more easily nudge it into place in Step 7.

6 Cut a 2" length of electrical tape, and use it to wrap over just the top and sides of the motor.

Gently position motor so that the rubber tube is over the flywheel   *Don't twist the motor too much!*

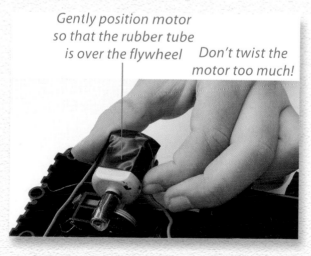

7 With the motor lightly held by the glue, carefully move the motor to align the shaft. You want it right over the friction wheel.

With motor in correct position, you can now glue it in place

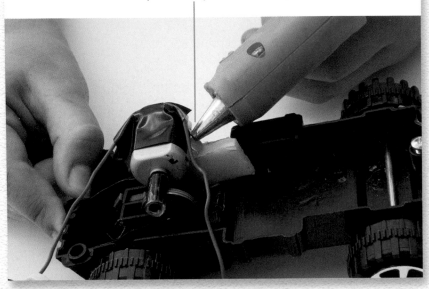

8 Apply more glue around the base of the motor to hold it permanently in place.

9 Cut two pieces of electrical tape to about 3" each.

10 Apply the first piece of tape over the top of the motor and onto the front floor of the car chassis.

11 Repeat with the second piece, this time applying the tape onto the back floor of the car chassis.

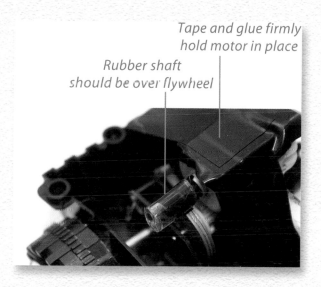

Tape and glue firmly
hold motor in place

Rubber shaft
should be over flywheel

When putting on the tape, check to make sure the rubber shaft of the motor is still firmly over the flywheel of the friction drive. Use the tape to keep the motor in the right position.

Be absolutely sure the exposed metal parts of the wires DO NOT touch each other or the metal case of the motor. Touching can cause a short circuit. Not only will this prevent the motor from working, but it also can overheat the battery and pose a potential safety risk.

TEST THE MOTOR WITH A BATTERY

You're almost done. Before finishing the electrical part of the robot, it's a good time to test the motor, its electrical connections, and its mounting. Everything needs to be working just right before your robot buggy will move:

1 **Raise the base of the car off your work table using an eraser or something else small and flat. You want the rear wheels to not touch your work table.**

2 **Touch the bare part of the wires to the top and bottom of a battery. The motor should turn (it's okay if it's a little slow), and the rear wheels should spin.**

Uh, oh! Nothing happened? Try these fixes:

» Be sure the battery is fresh. Use only new, fresh alkaline or heavy duty batteries.

» Check that the bare ends of the wires are touching the top and bottom terminals of the battery.

» Peel up the tape covering the motor terminals, and make sure the wires are still firmly in place.

Be absolutely sure the bare parts of the motor wires DO NOT touch each other or the metal case of the motor. Otherwise, this could cause a short circuit. Short circuits are bad news, m'kay?

Want a more permanent connection? Then you'll need to solder the wires onto the motor. Soldering involves working with a soldering iron, a tool that generates pin-point heat at about 700° Fahrenheit. That's mighty hot! Touching the wrong end of a soldering iron can cause very serious burns. Instant pain, blisters, and even scars. For this reason, none of the projects in this book require soldering.

Should you want to step up to soldering, I highly recommend you ask for help from a parent or other adult. The best way to discover soldering is to buy a soldering kit, available through numerous online sources. See "Finding the Stuff to Build Your Robots," at the back of this book, for suggestions about robot-making kits and parts.

CONNECT AND MOUNT THE BATTERIES

The completed toy robot buggy uses two AAA size batteries. The batteries are wired in *series* — that means one right after the other — in order to increase the voltage supplied to the motor.

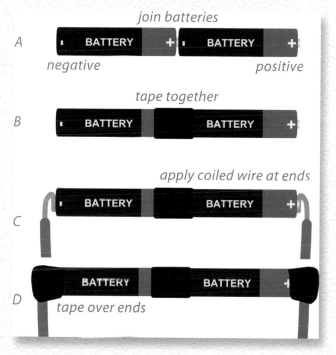

1. **Join two batteries in a row. The positive terminal of the bottom battery should connect with the negative terminal of the top battery.**

2. **Cut a 3" length of electrical tape.**

3. **Wrap the batteries together with the tape.**

4. **Check the direction the motor turns the wheels by *briefly* touching the bare wires to the top and bottom of the battery pack.**

If the car goes backwards, reverse the battery pack, and try again. Memorize how the wires connect to the battery in order to get the car going in the forward direction.

5 **Make small coils in the exposed ends. These will serve as battery connections.**

6 **Cut two 2" lengths of electrical tape.**

7 **For each of the two wires, position the coil in the center of the sticky side of the tape, then apply the tape to its nearby battery terminal.**

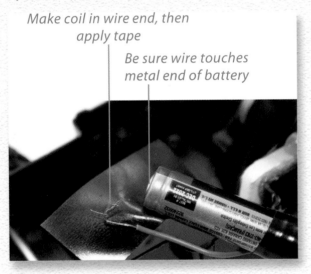

Make coil in wire end, then apply tape

Be sure wire touches metal end of battery

8 **Position the battery pack inside the car chassis, observing the orientation of the batteries that you checked in Step 3. On my car, the positive (+) terminal faced the rear of the car. Yours might be different, due to the way the motor and friction drive you use operate.**

When both wires are attached, the harder you press on the tape, the more likely the battery circuit will be completed, and the motor will run. When you release the tape, the connection will be broken, and the motor should stop.

9 Cut another piece of tape, this time about 3" long.

To turn motor on,
stretch rubber band
to other end of batteries

Wrapped ends hold wires to battery

And wrap rubber band on this end

10 On the end of the battery closest to the rear of the car, wrap a medium-size rubber band around the battery terminal, and hold it in place with the tape.

OF BATTERIES, MOTOR VOLTAGE, AND MOTOR POWER

A single non-rechargeable (alkaline or heavy duty) AAA battery provides about 1.5 volts (the exact voltage changes as the battery is used). At this voltage, the motor turns at a certain speed and provides a certain amount of turning power.

(continued)

(continued)

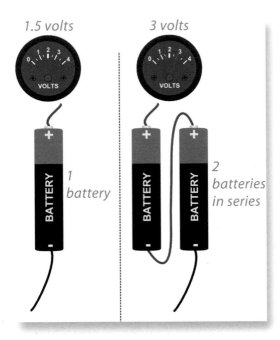

This speed and power may not be enough to actually move your robot across the floor. So, for this project, two AAA batteries are joined together in *series*. In this arrangement, the voltage from each cell is added together. Now the batteries produce a total of 3.0 volts. Very nifty.

The higher voltage not only increases the speed of the robot, it increases the amount of power that the motor can produce. Motor power is like the horsepower in a car: The higher the horsepower, the more the car is able to go faster, or to easily travel up hills.

I selected AAA-size batteries because they're small and lightweight and fit best in the car chassis. The bigger AA, C, and D cells are too big and heavy for the robot buggy project.

PLAYING WITH YOUR ROBOT BUGGY

Your new robot is now complete and ready for its performance trials!

Find a flat, smooth (uncarpeted) surface. A tiled kitchen floor is good.

Holding your robot in one hand, fingers away from the wheels or motor, stretch the rubber band to the other end of the battery pack. The band should squeeze the batteries together, and the motor should turn on.

Now, place the battery inside the chassis for a snug fit, put the robot on the ground, and let it go!

GOING FURTHER

Your self-propelled motorized buggy robot is super cool just as it is. But you can do even more with it! Here are a couple

of bonus projects you might want to try. Find them online at
www.robotpalace.com/byob/:

Some bonus projects may require help from an adult.
See the bonus project plans for details.

» **Add decorations.** Trick out your robotic car by adding
   cyalume glow sticks, small rave lights, self-contained light
   emitting diodes, glitter, googly eyeballs — anything that
   catches your fancy!

» **Add a battery holder.** Replace the taped-up batteries with a
   cozy two-cell battery holder. Just drop the batteries into the
   holder whenever they need to be replaced.

» **Add a shutoff switch.** Turn off the motor to your car if it
   runs into something.

PROJECT 3 BUILD A MOUSEBOT

ROBOTS ARE GREAT FOR ENTERTAINING PEOPLE. Correction, make that people *and* pets! The family feline or Fido may turn out to love robots just as much as you do.

In this project, you learn how to build a small, hyperactive robot that scurries across the floor. It's simple to make and requires just a few inexpensive parts you can find online. When you're done with construction, just place it on the floor, and watch out as the room comes alive in a frenzy of activity.

It's called a *mousebot* because the robot behaves a little like a mouse scurrying across the room. Set it down on any smooth floor, and it'll speed off in one direction, spin in circles, then bounce off walls and furniture and people before heading off in a new direction.

So what are we waiting for? Let the fun begin!

GETTING EVERYTHING ROUNDED UP

Unlike the first two projects, the mousebot *chassis* — that's just a fancy word for body — isn't built on a toy or other product. You make it from scratch using cheap and easy-to-find foam board. On this body, you glue on a couple of motors and a battery holder. Batteries go into the holder, and the robot goes into high gear!

MATERIALS YOU NEED

To complete this project, you need these materials:

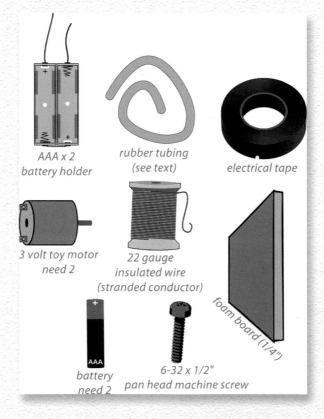

AAA x 2
battery holder

rubber tubing
(see text)

electrical tape

3 volt toy motor
need 2

22 gauge
insulated wire
(stranded conductor)

foam board (1/4")

battery
need 2

6-32 x 1/2"
pan head machine screw

2 Small 1.5-to-3 volt toy motors (see "Finding the Stuff to Build Your Robots" at the back of the book)

1 Roll of electrical tape

1 foot 22 gauge stranded wire

1 AAAx2 battery holder (for AAA batteries; try to get the kind with wires already attached)

2 AAA alkaline, heavy duty flashlight, or rechargeable batteries

1 6-32 x 1/2" pan head machine screw (see text for details)

1" 1/4" diameter (outside dimension) clear tubing; this tubing is about 3/16" inside dimension — aquarium (fish tank) tube is okay, but be sure it's the clear, soft kind

5" by 5" Foam board or thick cardboard

TOOLS YOU NEED

To complete this project, you need these tools:

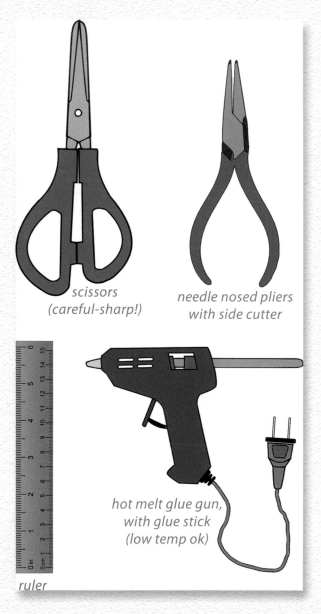

scissors
(careful-sharp!)

needle nosed pliers
with side cutter

hot melt glue gun,
*with glue stick
(low temp ok)*

ruler

Hot melt glue gun and glue stick

Scissors, for cutting foam board and electrical tape

Needle nosed pliers with a side cutter, or wire cutters

Ruler, for measuring the lengths of things

SPARE MOTORS OR USING NEW?

In Project 2, I wrote about how to find small motors in discarded toys. That's a great way to save money, and it works fine for the buggy robot in that project.

But for the mousebot, it's better to get two new motors because then you know they are the same. Don't worry — you can buy them for under $2 each from many online sources. See "Finding the Stuff to Build Your Robots," at the back of this book, for more details.

These motors look much the same on the outside… but they are different inside

Why is it important to know what kind of motors you have? Small toy motors can look the same on the outside, but inside they might be wired differently. This can cause them to rotate at different speeds. One motor may turn

(continued)

(continued)

at 6,000 revolutions per minute (*RPM*), whereas another that looks exactly the same may go at 10,000 RPM.

Mousebot uses two motors, one on each side. If the motors turn at greatly different speeds, your robot will only spin in very tight circles and may never go in a straight line.

MAKING THE MOUSEBOT

With all the parts in hand, you're ready to make your mousebot.

ADD A RUBBER "TIRE" TO THE MOTOR SHAFTS

You already read that mousebot uses two motors, one on each side. The metal shafts of the motors need to have a rubber "tire" added around them. This gives the mousebot better traction as it skims across the floor.

This is done by wrapping several layers of electrical tape around the shaft and then sticking on a short piece of clear tubing, the kind used for supplying air in fish tanks:

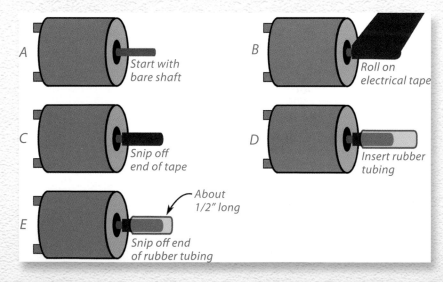

A — Start with bare shaft

B — Roll on electrical tape

C — Snip off end of tape

D — Insert rubber tubing

E — Snip off end of rubber tubing — About 1/2" long

1   Cut two pieces of electrical tape to 1-1/2"

2   Carefully apply one of the tape pieces to the shaft. Slowly spin the shaft as the tape rolls onto it. Go slowly, and be sure the tape goes on straight!

3   Apply the second piece of tape in the same way.

Rolling the tape onto the motor shaft takes some practice. Be sure there aren't any crimps or crinkles in the tape. If you make a mistake, peel off the bad tape, and try again with a new piece.

4   Use scissors to snip off the extra tape at the end of the shaft.

5   Cut a piece of aquarium tubing to about 3/4" length.

6   Wet both the tubing and the electrical tape (to make them slippery), and carefully push the tubing over the taped motor shaft.

7   Snip off the end of the tubing so there's about 1/4" extra beyond the motor shaft. The rubber tubing should be about 1/2" long.

8   Repeat Steps 1 through 7 for the other motor. Remember, you need two!

Don't cut the tubing too short! If you do, then when the motor is mounted on the robot, the "tires" may not properly touch the ground.

ATTACH WIRES TO THE MOTORS

Do your motors already have wires already connected to them, and are these wires at least 4" long? If you answered yes, you're done with this part. Otherwise, follow these steps.

If you built the buggy robot in Project 2, you'll already know what to do because the steps here are nearly the same. They are repeated here so you don't have to flip pages back and forth.

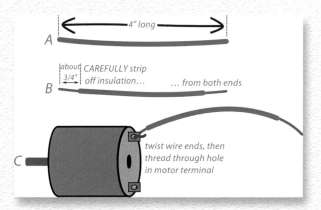

1 Use needle nosed pliers with a side cutter (the cutting blade is part of the pliers) to cut two pieces of wire, each to a length of 4".

2 Use the pliers to *carefully* trim off 3/4" of insulation from the ends of both wires. Work carefully. Remove *only* the insulation, without cutting into the wire.

3 Use your fingers to twist the wire strands into a tight braid.

4 Take one of the wires and push it through an eyelet terminal on the motor. Thread it halfway, then twist the wire back around itself. This makes the wire-to-terminal connection as tight as possible.

5 Do the same for the other eyelet terminal on the motor.

6 Now cut two pieces of electrical tape to 1-1/2".

7 For each motor, apply the tape over the eyelet terminals to keep the wires in place.

USING A WIRE STRIPPING TOOL

Needle nosed pliers and even scissors or wire cutters can be used for cutting and stripping off the ends of wires, but they aren't the ideal tools for this job.

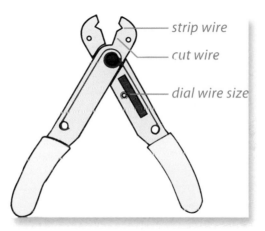

strip wire

cut wire

dial wire size

So what is? A *wire stripper*. This has funny-looking cutting jaws that strip off only the outer insulation without cutting the wire itself. Most also have a cutter edge for snipping the wires.

(continued)

(continued)

> To use a wire stripper tool, you must first "dial in" the gauge of the wire you're using. Wire gauge is the diameter of the wire. We're using 22 gauge for the mousebot, so dial the wire diameter to 22.
>
> To use, just place the tool near the end of the wire, close the jaws, and pull. The insulation comes right off! Easy-peasy.

CUT THE BASE PIECE

The (chassis) body of the mousebot is simple, consisting of a small base and four 1" square pieces that serve as motor mounts. All of it is cut from 1/4" foam board.

Start by using scissors to:

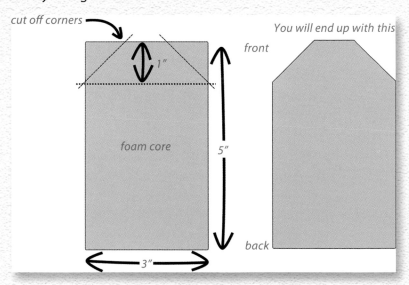

cut off corners

You will end up with this

front

1"

foam core

5"

3"

back

1 **Cut a 3" by 5" piece of foam board.**

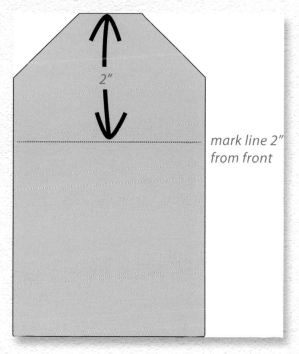

2"

mark line 2"
from front

2 **Mark a line across the base 2" from one end. This end will be the "front" of the robot.**

3 **Clip off the corners in the front to make a kind of arrow shape.**

That's all for now. We'll make those 1" square pieces as we go along in the next set of steps.

MOUNT THE MOTORS

Now it's time to mount the motors to the mousebot. Time to get out your hot melt glue gun!

All the projects in this book are assembled using a low temperature hot melt glue gun. These operate at a lower temperature than a standard glue gun, but they still do an excellent job of holding things together.

But — and this is very important — to get the most out of the glue gun, be sure to let it heat up completely before using it. If you don't, the glue won't hold very well, and your project may fall apart. Give your glue gun at least five minutes to reach full temperature.

You can get burned even when using a low temperature glue gun. Allow at least 20 seconds for any glue to cool before touching it. Never touch the metal tip of the glue gun with your fingers. If you need to remove excess glue from the tip, use a paper towel.

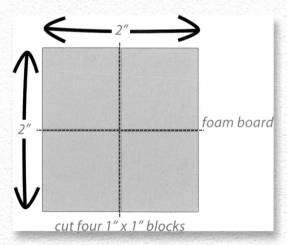

foam board

cut four 1" x 1" blocks

1 **Cut four small squares of foam board to about 1" by 1".**

2 On each square, use a pen to mark a line right down its middle.

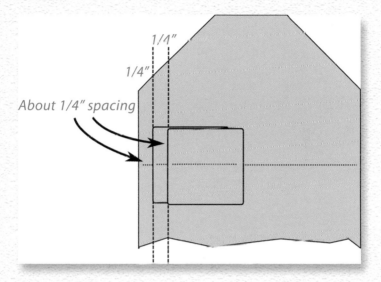

1/4"

1/4"

About 1/4" spacing

3 Take one square and position it so its marked line matches with the line on the robot base. Place the bottom square about 1/4" in from the edge of the base. Mark its position with a pen, then glue into place with the hot glue gun.

4 Repeat for the top square. Place it about 1/4" in from the edge of the square beneath it. Check the position, mark with a pen, and then glue in place with the hot glue gun.

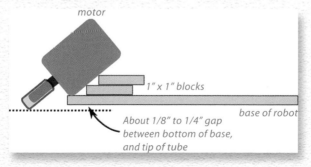

motor

1" x 1" blocks

base of robot

About 1/8" to 1/4" gap between bottom of base, and tip of tube

5 Take one motor and place it at an angle along the edges of the foam board. The tip of the rubber tube tire should stick down below the bottom of the base by about 1/8" or 1/4" — not too much, not too little.

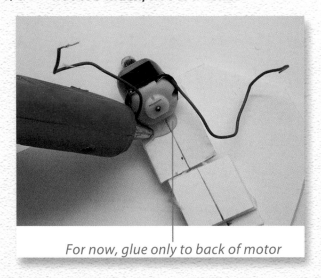

For now, glue only to back of motor

6 Apply hot melt glue between the back of the motor and the top square.

7 Repeat Steps 3 through 6 for the other motor on the other side of the robot.

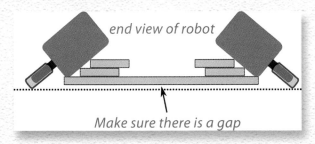

end view of robot

Make sure there is a gap

8 Put your mousebot on a flat surface and verify that the front of the base is off the ground. When you're sure, apply more glue around the edges of the motors to stick them on better. If you need to adjust the distance the rubber tires stick out from the bottom of the robot, make the adjustment now.

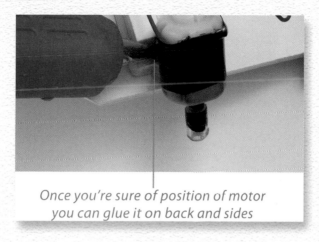

Once you're sure of position of motor you can glue it on back and sides

9 **Things lookin' good? Great! Finish mounting the motors by applying more glue all around the sides and under the front.**

Be absolutely sure the tip of the rubber tube sticks below the bottom of the base by about 1/8" to 1/4". If it doesn't, your mousebot may not have any traction to move! It's better to err on the side of extra distance than not enough.

ADD A "TAIL"

The rear end of the mousebot uses a kind of "tail" to keep the back side of the robot from scraping the floor. It's just a 6-32 x 1/2" long machine screw glued in place.

As noted in the parts list, be sure this screw has a pan or round head. Don't use a flat head screw. The roundness of the screw head makes for a better surface to glide over.

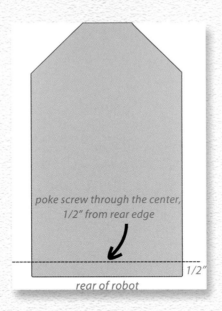

poke screw through the center,
1/2" from rear edge

1/2"

rear of robot

1 Use your ruler to mark a spot 1/2" from the back edge of the mousebot, halfway between the right and left side.

2 Use a pen to poke a hole at this spot.

3 Push the machine screw through the hole from the underside of the base.

Apply a light amount of glue to the machine screw to hold it in place

4 Secure the screw in place by dabbing on a bit of hot melt glue to the top (thread portion) of the screw.

You can use the screw to attach things to your mousebot, like a piece of string or a bell.

TEST EACH MOTOR WITH A BATTERY

Before completing construction of the mousebot, now is a good time to test each motor to make sure all is working. Now is also the time to determine which way the motors turn when connected to the battery:

1 **Place your mousebot on something — a cup, say, or a short glass — so that the motor shafts aren't touching anything.**

2 **Position the robot so that the arrow shape points away from you. This helps you determine the "right" and "left" side of the mousebot.**

3 **Touch the bare end of one of the wires to the + (positive) terminal of an AAA battery. Touch the other wire to the – (negative) terminal of the battery. The motor should spin.**

If nothing happens, try these remedies:

» Use only new, fresh batteries.

» Check that the bare ends of the wires are touching the top and bottom terminals of the battery.

» Peel up the tape covering the motor terminals and make sure the wires are still firmly in place.

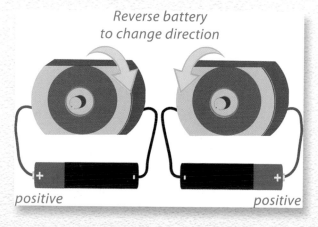

Reverse battery to change direction

positive　　*positive*

4 Observe which direction the motor turns. For the motor on the right side, it needs to turn *clockwise*. If it doesn't, reverse the wires to the battery and try again.

5 Mark the wire that goes to the + battery terminal by sticking a small piece of electrical tape anywhere along its length.

6 Repeat Steps 2 through 4 for the other motor, except this time check that the motor turns *counter-clockwise*.

7 With the motor verified to turn counter-clockwise, use electrical tape to mark the wire that goes to the + battery terminal.

WIRE THE BATTERY HOLDER

The mousebot is powered by two AAA batteries. To make it easier to construct and play with the mousebot, use a two-cell battery holder.

The best kind of holder to get is the type with wires already connected to it. The wires should be at least 2" long.

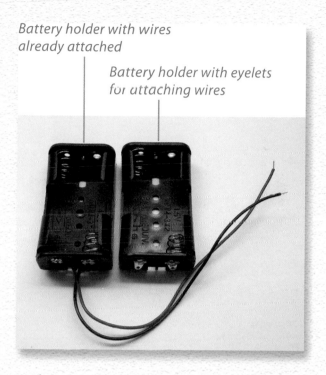

Battery holder with wires already attached

Battery holder with eyelets for attaching wires

TIP

If you can't find a battery holder with wires already attached, the kind with small eyelets for the wires is okay. With these, you can wire up the motors directly to the battery holder.

If your battery holder is the kind with wires already attached:

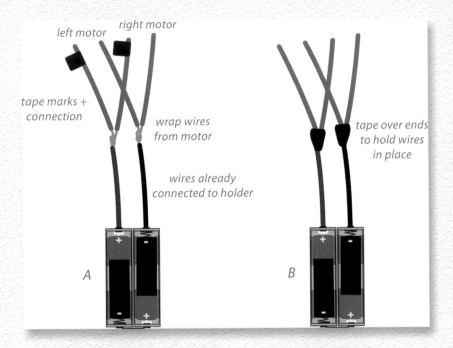

left motor

right motor

tape marks +
connection

wrap wires
from motor

tape over ends
to hold wires
in place

wires already
connected to holder

A

B

1 Twist together both of the motor wires from the previous set of steps that you marked with the electrical tape. These wires join with the red (+, positive) terminal of the battery holder.

2 Twist together the remaining two motor wires. These wires join with the black (–, negative) terminal of the battery holder.

3 Cut two 1" lengths of electrical tape.

4 Wrap the tape around the exposed wires to keep them in place and to prevent them from touching one another.

If your battery holder is the kind with eyelet tabs instead of wires:

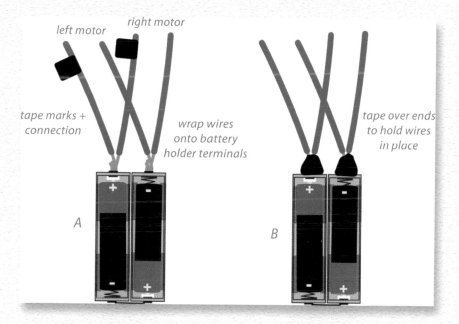

left motor

right motor

tape marks +
connection

wrap wires
onto battery
holder terminals

tape over ends
to hold wires
in place

A

B

1 Twist together both of the motor wires from the previous set of steps that you marked with the electrical tape. Thread these wires into the + eyelet. Twist them around the eyelet to make a solid connection.

2 Twist together the remaining two motor wires. Thread these wires into the – eyelet, and twist them around the eyelet for a solid connection.

3 Cut two 1" lengths of electrical tape.

4 Wrap the tape around the eyelets to keep the wires in place.

Be sure the metal parts of the wires DO NOT touch each other or the metal case of the motor. Touching can cause a short circuit. If this happens, the motor won't work, and the batteries may become very hot.

MOUNT THE BATTERY HOLDER

You don't want the mousebot batteries to spill out on the floor when the robot is in action. Keep things in place by physically mounting the battery holder to the base of the robot.

Apply two dabs of hot melt glue to the bottom of the battery holder, and then stick the holder to the top of the mousebot base. There's more than enough room for the holder to go between the motors and the tail screw.

RECHARGEABLE OR NON-RECHARGEABLE?

Motorized robots are power hungry. They can drain a set of batteries in no time flat. Instead of popping in a new set of expensive alkaline batteries each time you play with the mousebot, consider using rechargeable cells instead.

Just know that if you do switch out to rechargeable batteries, it's quite normal for the motors to run a little slower. Why is this so?

The average voltage from an alkaline (or heavy duty) battery is 1.5 volts. But for a rechargeable cell it's only 1.2 volts. When placed in a battery holder, the voltage from each cell is added together. The sum voltage from two alkaline batteries is 3 volts (2 x 1.5 volts).

By comparison, the sum voltage from rechargeable cells (2 x 1.2 volts) is 2.4 volts, over half a volt less. With lower voltage, the motors run a little slower. That's okay for the mousebot, because it's already pretty zippy.

The two main rechargeable batteries on the market today are nickel metal hydride (abbreviated NiMH) and nickel cadmium (abbreviated NiCad). It doesn't matter which you use, but be sure you have the proper recharger for your type of batteries. Using the wrong kind of recharger could wreck them.

PLAYING WITH THE MOUSEBOT

You're almost done building your mousebot!

Collect two fresh AAA battery cells. FInd a flat, smooth (uncarpeted) surface — the tiled floor in the kitchen is a good spot.

Load the batteries into the battery holder. Be sure to insert them properly: the + side of each battery must line up with the + symbol on the holder. When all the batteries are in, the mousebot motors should scream into action!

Warn everyone in your house that a wild robot is about to run loose. Put the mousebot on the ground, and step back!

Invariably the mousebot will get caught up with some object — a wall, a chair leg, maybe even you! Be ready to help it out by moving it to a new spot.

HEY, MY MOUSEBOT ONLY SPINS IN CIRCLES!

Crazy spinning is what mousebot does, but it's also supposed to occasionally go straight, veer off in the occasional gnarly right turn, and maybe surprise you with a sudden left hook from time to time.

Alas, yours only spins in tight circles, like a whacked-out Disneyland Mad Tea Party ride. So what's wrong? Here are some possibilities:

» **A motor is turning in the wrong direction.** The motors on the mousebot — like any similar two-wheeled robot — need to turn in *opposite* directions. One goes clockwise, the other goes counter-clockwise.

» **The motors aren't matched.** Though they look the same on the outside, the two motors must be the same kind or they might spin at drastically different speeds.

» **One of the motors isn't turning at all.** If a motor isn't on, check its wiring.

> » **Something's caught in the motor shaft and slowing it down.** Clean out any junk there and try again.

Here's another problem you may encounter: Your robot runs backward — it thinks the tail end (with the machine screw) is the front. This is caused when the motor wires are connected backward to the battery holder.

If either problem happens, rewire the connection to the battery holder so that:

> » The right motor turns clockwise.

> » The left motor turns counter-clockwise.

To make your mousebot stop, just pull out one of its batteries.

GOING FURTHER

You're probably interested in some enhancements you can make to your mousebot. Check these out online at www.robotpalace.com/byob/:

Some bonus projects may require help from an adult. See the bonus project plans for details.

» **Add a streaming tail and other decoration.** Personalize your mousebot by drawing or coloring on it and adding bling to its body and tail.

» **Make an army of mousebots and let them all loose at the same time.** For your extra bots, you can skip the measuring and download a template at www.dummies.com/go/buildingyourownrobots.

PROJECT 4 HACK A RADIO-CONTROLLED TOY

THE TERM "HACKING" USED TO BE A GOOD THING. It still is, when it means tearing some hardware thingamabob apart, discovering how it works, then rebuilding it into something fresh and exciting.

Radio-controlled toys are a hardware hacker's goldmine. With just a screwdriver and some odds-and-ends, you can turn yesterday's junk into today's robot learning platform.

Use your platform to discover more advanced things about robotics, things like directly controlling the motors to move your robot, the many ways robots steer and drive, and much more.

That's precisely where we're headed with this project: You learn how to find and identify likely R/C toy candidates for hacking, how to take the contraption apart, and how to transform its motors into your first fully fledged robotic invention system.

This project is designed around toy R/C vehicles, the kind you can buy new for under $25. Leave the expensive radio-controlled race cars alone.

FINDING RADIO-CONTROLLED TOYS FOR ROBOT FORGING

You can purchase a new (inexpensive) toy, or find one at a yard sale, thrift shop — maybe even your own closet.

THE GOOD, THE BAD, AND THE NOT SO PRETTY

Not all R/C toys are well-suited to turning them into robots. Things to look for:

» **Full function.** You want a radio-controlled toy that gives you independent control over its movement: forward, backward, and steering. Some toys only steer when they are put in reverse. Don't bother with these.

» **Reasonable speed.** Some R/C toys are built for racing. Although they're fun as radio-controlled toys, these move too fast to be useful as robots. A lumbering 4x4 toy truck is ideal!

» **Decent condition.** If your candidate toy is used, check for damage that might make it inoperable. Open its battery compartment, and give it a pass if the batteries have leaked.

You won't be using the remote control unit when hacking the vehicle, so things like the radio frequency aren't important. In fact, you don't even need the remote. If you're scouring garage sales and resale shops, it's okay if the remote is long lost.

STEERING STYLES

Toy R/C vehicles — and robots, too — move and turn using a number of techniques. Here are the three most common:

» **Two-function.** There's only one motor in toys like this. When going forward the car goes straight;

when backing up, it turns. As noted above, give this type of vehicle a pass.

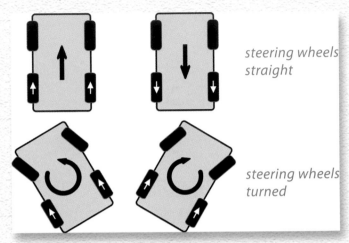

steering wheels straight

steering wheels turned

» **Full-function car-type.** The toy has two motors. One motor drives the rear wheels and makes the toy go forward and back. The other motor turns the front steering wheels right or left, just like in a car.

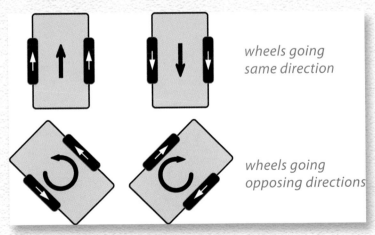

wheels going same direction

wheels going opposing directions

» **Full-function differential.** This kind of R/C toy has two motors, one for each drive wheel. The direction of each wheel determines how the toy moves:

  » Both wheels spin forward: vehicle moves forward

» Both wheels spin in reverse: vehicle moves backward

» Wheels spin in alternate directions: vehicle turns to a new direction

With two-wheeled differential steering, one or more undriven wheels are commonly used for balance. These wheels are not part of the driving or steering mechanism, and are just there to keep the vehicle from tipping over.

TWO EXAMPLES OF HACKABLE R/C TOYS

In preparing this book, I wanted to show currently available R/C toys that lent themselves to robo hacks. I found numerous examples, all under $15, at local superstores and discount mail order outlets. I'll use just one of them in this project, but it's nice to know there's a variety available.

Don't get caught up with brands and models. Most R/C toys tend to have similar construction and parts inside, so if you can't find toys exactly like mine, odds are you'll find something else just as good.

R/C car using car-type steering

This traditional R/C truck uses car-type steering. One motor drives the rear wheels, which make it go back and forth. A second motor makes the front wheels turn right or left, causing the vehicle to turn.

R/C car using differential steering

This "tumbling" toy drives and spins on two oversized wheels. It's a good example of a differentially steered vehicle, the kind whose separate control sticks on the remote control make it move in all directions.

HACKING THE CAR-TYPE R/C TOY

Let's start by pulling apart a jeep styled R/C toy, which uses car-type steering. In this project, you begin by taking the toy apart and locating the wiring that goes to the two motors.

In place of the radio remote, you build your own homebrew switch using just foam board and miscellaneous hardware from the home improvement store. With this switch, you control the drive motor via wire, making the toy go forward and back.

This particular toy was made by New Bright, a major importer of inexpensive radio control toys. I bought mine at the local Wal-Mart for about $14.

MATERIALS YOU NEED

To complete this part of the project, you need these materials:

THE METHOD TO THIS MADNESS

Why bother pulling apart a perfectly good R/C toy and its remote control link, so you can add a mechanical switch for driving it around? Fair question. Here are three far-reaching answers:

» **It's a good way to explore the art and skill of hardware hacking.** We all learn best by actually doing it.

» **You'll discover one of the most important concepts of robotics: namely, how to reverse the direction that a motor turns using mechanical or electronic means.** Reversing a motor allows robots to move around their environment.

» **The wired switch is just the first step in modifying an R/C car to make a robot.** When you've mastered these basics, you can move on to adding a fully electronic brain, turning your once–human-operated toy into a self-guiding, intelligent robot.

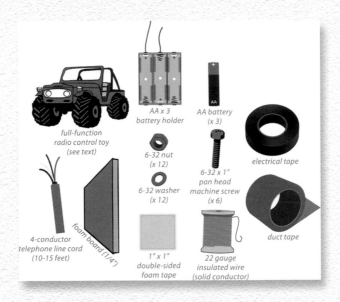

1 Radio-controlled toy vehicle, with car-type steering (see text)

1 Roll of electrical tape

1 Roll of duct tape

4 feet 22 gauge solid wire

1 10 to 15 feet of modular phone cord, four conductor

1 AAx3-battery holder (size AA; try to get the kind with wires already attached)

3 AA alkaline batteries

6 6-32 x 1" pan head machine screws

12 6-32 nuts

12 #6 flat washers

1" x 1" Double-sided foam tape

12" x 12" Foam board

TOOLS YOU NEED

To complete this part of the project, you need these tools:

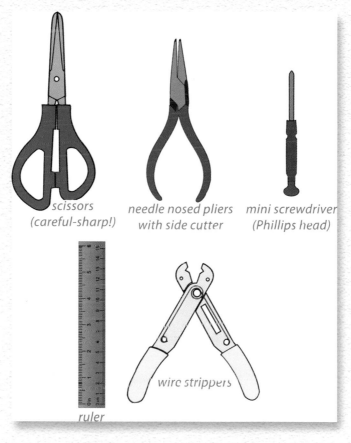

scissors
(careful-sharp!)

needle nosed pliers
with side cutter

mini screwdriver
(Phillips head)

ruler

wire strippers

Scissors, for cutting foam board and tape

Needle nosed pliers with a side cutter

Small Phillips screwdriver

Wire strippers

Ruler, for measuring the lengths of things

DISASSEMBLE THE TOY CAR

The first step of any hardware hacking project is to take the hardware apart:

If you have a matching remote control for your toy car, prior to taking anything apart, install batteries into both the car and remote, and test for proper operation. If something doesn't work, you may need to pick a different toy.

1 **Remove the outside body pieces of the car to expose the electronics and wiring inside.**

Almost all R/C toys are assembled using small Phillips screws — the kind of screw with the X-shaped slots in the head. Use a small screwdriver to take out the screws.

Be sure to remove all the screws! Otherwise the body won't come off easily, and you could break things. Some screws may be hidden in recessed areas, or covered up by paper decals.

2 **Additional decorative pieces may snap into place. Remove these by gently prying them away from the main chassis (body) of the toy.**

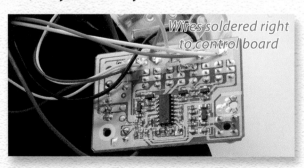

Wires soldered right to control board

5 Look for the motor wiring. On some toys, the wiring is soldered directly to the electronic control board. For these, you need to use wire cutters to snip the wires from the control board. (Don't do this part yet!)

Wires plugged in with connectors

4 On some toys, as with the example car-type toy, the motors plug in using connectors. Gently pry the connections apart. No wire cutting is necessary. Yea!

CUT THE PARTS FOR THE SWITCH AND CONTROL BASE

The control base and switch for your hacked R/C car is made out of 1/4" foam board:

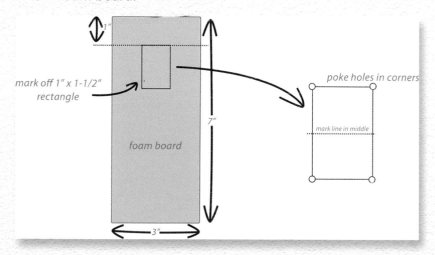

1"

mark off 1" x 1-1/2" rectangle

poke holes in corners

mark line in middle

7"

foam board

3"

1 Cut a 3" x 7" piece of foam board. This is the *switch base*.

2 Near one end of the base, use a pen to mark off a rectangle 1" by 1-1/2".

3 Use your pen to mark a line half way down the middle of the rectangle.

4 Use a small Phillips screwdriver to poke holes at the four corners of the rectangle. These are starter holes for the machine screws, explained next.

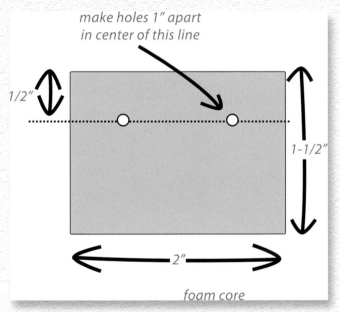

make holes 1" apart
in center of this line

1/2"

1-1/2"

2"

foam core

5 Cut a rectangular piece of foam board that measures 2" by 1-1/2" inches. This is the *switch plate*.

6 Mark a line 1/2" from the long edge of the piece you cut in Step 5.

7 Along the center of this line, use the Phillips screwdriver to poke two holes, 1" apart.

CONSTRUCT THE SWITCH

The homemade switch uses common 6-32 hardware from the home improvement store. There are several steps to go through, but it's all pretty straightforward. You'll start by adding metal hardware to the switch base:

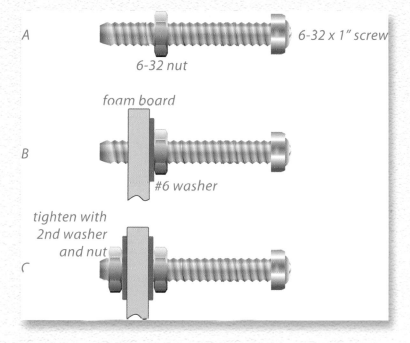

A — 6-32 nut — 6-32 x 1" screw

B — foam board — #6 washer

C — tighten with 2nd washer and nut

1 **Thread a nut about a third of the way of the onto a 6-32 x 1" screw.**

We'll call this the *top nut*.

2 **Place a #6 washer onto the screw, and then push the screw into one of the four holes on the switch base.**

3 Place another #6 washer onto the screw and secure the screw in place with a second nut.

This is the *bottom nut*.

4 Thread the bottom nut so that about 1/8" of the end of the screw pokes through.

5 Repeat Steps 1 through 4 for the remaining screws, nuts, and washers.

Let's now turn to the switch plate:

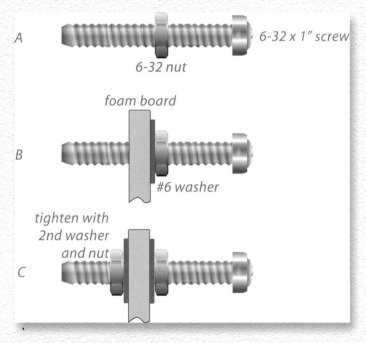

A — 6-32 x 1" screw

6-32 nut

foam board

B

#6 washer

tighten with
2nd washer
and nut

C

1 Thread a nut about half way onto a 6-32 x 1" screw (again, the *top nut*).

2 Place a #6 washer onto the screw and push the screw into one of the holes in the switch plate.

3 Place another #6 washer onto the screw and secure the screw in place with a second nut (*bottom nut*).

4 Thread the bottom nut so that the front and back of the screw have about the same length.

5 Loosely tighten the screw in place by turning the top nut.

6 Repeat Steps 1 through 5 for the other screw, nut, and washer.

Apply duct tape to make a hinge (apply both sides)

7 Cut two 1" lengths of duct tape.

8 Place the switch plate over the line you previously drew between the screw posts.

9 Apply a 1" length of duct tape to one side of the switch plate. The tape should be a little loose at the bottom.

10 Apply a second 1" length of duct tape to the other side of the switch plate. Again, make the tape a little loose.

You should be able to rock the switch plate back and forth to about 45 degrees on either side. If the duct tape is applied too tightly, the plate may have restricted motion. Simply peel off one or both pieces of tape and try again.

11 Visually test the switch by rocking it forward and backward — the screws in the moving part of the switch should touch their respective screws front and back. Use a screwdriver to make any fine-tuning adjustments.

WIRE THE SWITCH TO CREATE AN "H-BRIDGE" CIRCUIT

In previous projects, you learned that you can reverse the direction of a motor by changing its connections to the battery. Flip the wiring to make the motor go the other way. The change in battery polarity makes the motor go into reverse.

Reversing a motor by disconnecting and then reconnecting its wiring is fine for testing, but it makes for a cumbersome robot. To the rescue: the *H-bridge circuit*. Using a switch like the one you just made, you can arrange the wiring to easily change the polarity of the battery to the motor.

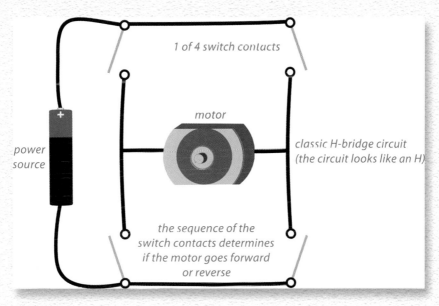

1 of 4 switch contacts

motor

power
source

classic H-bridge circuit
(the circuit looks like an H)

the sequence of the
switch contacts determines
if the motor goes forward
or reverse

TIP

*This method of wiring is called an H-bridge because
the connections kinda-sorta look like an H.*

The type of switch you made is called a *double-pole, double-throw*
switch, or *DPDT* for short. You need this kind of switch to form
the H-bridge.

With the aid of the DPDT switch, flip the switch one way and
current from a battery flows through the motor in a certain
direction. It's the direction of this current that determines how
the motor spins. Flip the switch the other way, and the current
flows through the motor the other way. Presto-magico, the motor
spins the other way. (Actually, it's not magic at all, but physics.)

Wiring the switch to make an H-bridge circuit is easy: Just add
two wires on the underside of the switch to form a cross-cross.

Current is the flow of electric charge. This charge is created by electrons, a basic subatomic particle. The more electrons that flow, the higher the current. With higher currents, motors produce more force so they can do bigger and better things. You can learn more about current in any good book on electronics.

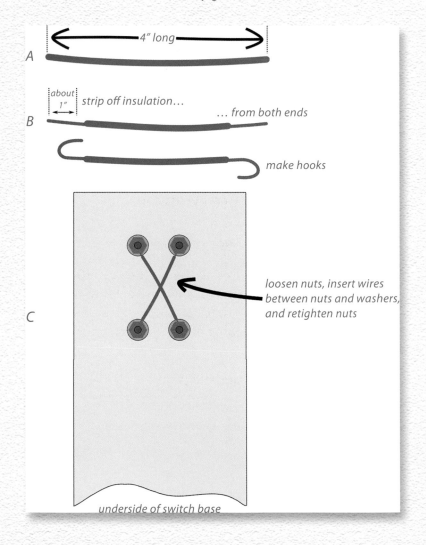

A ←———— 4" long ————→

B about 1" strip off insulation…
… from both ends

make hooks

C loosen nuts, insert wires between nuts and washers, and retighten nuts

underside of switch base

1 Cut two pieces of solid conductor wire, each to 4".

2 On the ends of both pieces, strip off 1" of insulation. Make little hook shapes in the exposed wiring.

 Use the shaft of your screwdriver as a form for making the wire hooks.

3 Turn the switch base upside down to expose the nut-and-screw terminals. Take a wire, and loosen one of the nuts. Place a wire hook between the nut and washer and retighten.

4 Connect the other end of this wire to the nut-and-screw terminal in the opposite corner.

5 Repeat Steps 3 and 4 for the other wire, using the two remaining nuts-and-screw terminals.

WIRE THE SWITCH TO THE MOTOR

Your DPDT switch is hardwired to the motor. Even though the drive motor needs just two wires, you connect it to the R/C toy using a telephone line cord that has four wires inside it. The extra wires are for future expansion, needed later in the chapter.

Some phone line cords have just two wires in them. You can tell this by looking at the modular plugs on the ends of the cord. The plugs should have four metal contacts, not just two.

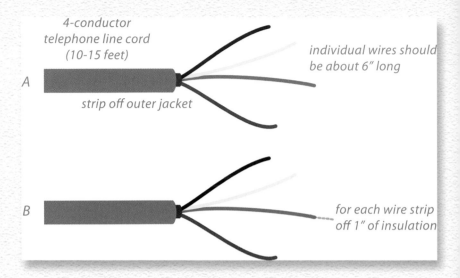

4-conductor
telephone line cord
(10-15 feet)

*individual wires should
be about 6" long*

A

strip off outer jacket

B

*for each wire strip
off 1" of insulation*

1 Cut the plug ends off a 10- to 15-foot-long telephone line cord.

2 Use a pair of wire cutters to remove 6" of the outer jacket of each end of the line cord.

Don't try to do this with simple wire cutters or you'll end up chopping into the wires inside. A pair of wire strippers is the much better tool. To prevent nicking the inside wires, set the cutter to 12 or 14 gauge, big enough to just remove the outer jacket of the phone cord, but not cut into any of the separate wires inside.

3 Now set the wire stripper for 22 or 24 gauge wire. Use the tool to strip off 1" of insulation from each of the four wires. (Note: Telephone wire can be even smaller than 22 or 24 gauge. If yours is, dial the smallest gauge you have available and do your best.)

4 Slightly loosen one of the nuts at the top end of the switch plate.

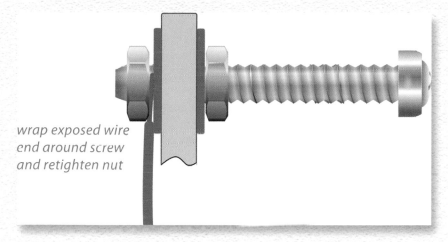

wrap exposed wire end around screw and retighten nut

5 Pick one of the colored wires in the phone cord and twist the wires to keep the strands together.

6 Wrap the exposed phone cord wire around the screw, between the nut and washer. Retighten the nut.

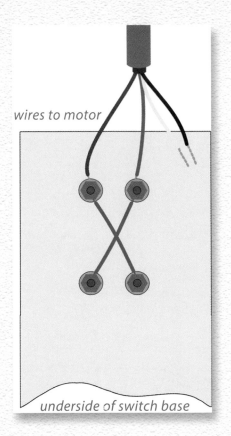

wires to motor

underside of switch base

7 **Pick another of the colored wires from the phone cord and repeat Steps 4 through 6 for the other nut at the top end of the switch plate.**

It takes a little practice to get both the telephone wires and crisscross wires on the same screw post. Be patient and work slowly — you'll get it!

ATTACH THE WIRES TO THE R/C CAR MOTOR

You're now ready to connect the other end of the telephone cord wires to the drive motor on your R/C car.

If the wires to the motors in your R/C toy use connectors, and you want to keep the connectors:

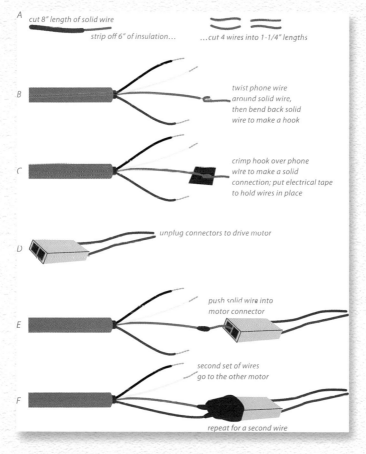

A cut 8" length of solid wire
strip off 6" of insulation…   …cut 4 wires into 1-1/4" lengths

B twist phone wire around solid wire, then bend back solid wire to make a hook

C crimp hook over phone wire to make a solid connection; put electrical tape to hold wires in place

D unplug connectors to drive motor

E push solid wire into motor connector

F second set of wires go to the other motor
repeat for a second wire

1 Cut an 8" length of solid conductor wire and remove at least 6" of insulation from it.

2 Cut the exposed wire into four equal lengths (about 1-1/4" each).

3 Use color coding to identify the two wires you used in the previous steps.

4 Take one of the wires and wrap the exposed metal conductors around half of the 1" bare wire.

5 Bend this end to make a hook in the wire. Use a pair of needle nosed pliers to crimp the wires together.

6 Cut a 1/2" length of electrical tape and wrap it around the wire leads to keep them in place.

7 Repeat Steps 3 through 6 for the other color-coded wire.

8 Unplug the drive motor connector in the R/C vehicle, if you haven't already.

9 Stick the bare ends of the two wires into the connector that leads to the drive motor.

If any of the bare wire sticks out of the plug, remove the wire and trim off a little to make it shorter. Avoid having any exposed part of the wire sticking out of the plug; a dangerous short circuit could occur if the wires touch.

10 Cut a length of 1" electrical tape and wrap it around the plug and wires to keep everything in place.

If the wires to the motors in your R/C toy are soldered directly to the toy's control board:

1 Identify the wires that go to the drive motor. (These are the wires that go to the rear of the toy, where the drive motor is placed.)

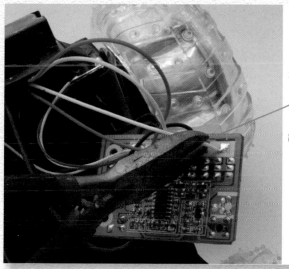

Clip off wires close to the control board

(Tip: After cutting, keep wires grouped together; it'll help you pair up which wires go to which motors!)

2 Use a pair of wire clippers to snip off the motor wires close to the circuit board.

3 For each of these two wires, strip off 1" of insulation.

4 Use color coding to identify the phone cord wires you used in the previous steps.

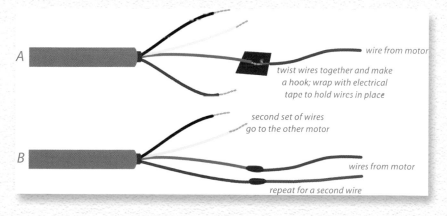

A

wire from motor

twist wires together and make a hook; wrap with electrical tape to hold wires in place

second set of wires go to the other motor

B

wires from motor

repeat for a second wire

5 Take one of these phone cord wires and wrap it together with one of the motor wires.

6 Bend the wires to make a hook, and use a pair of needle nosed pliers to crimp the wires together.

7 Cut a length of 1/2" electrical tape and wrap it around the wire leads to keep them in place.

8 Repeat Steps 4 through 7 for the other color-coded wire.

 Prevent the phone cord from being easily pulled out of the R/C toy by strapping the wire down with a strip or two of duct tape. While you're at it, turn the switch over, and apply a 2" to 3" length of duct tape to the wires to prevent them from pulling loose.

WIRE THE BATTERY HOLDER

The hacked R/C car is powered by three AA batteries held together conveniently in a three-cell battery holder. The batteries in the R/C toy aren't used.

 The best kind of holder to get is the type with wires already connected to them. The wires should be at least 3" long. If you can't find a battery holder with wires already attached, the kind with small eyelets for the wires is okay. With these, you can wire up the motors directly to the battery holder.

1 Strip 1" of insulation from both the red and black battery holder wires.

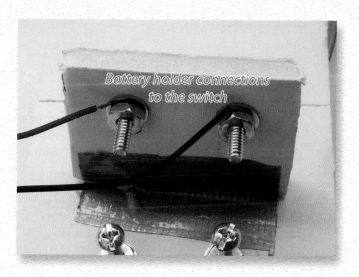

Battery holder connections to the switch

2 Take the red wire and twist the strands to keep them together. Loosen one of the bottom nuts on the switch plate screw terminals and attach the red wire to it.

3 Repeat for the black wire, using the other screw terminal on the switch plate.

Be sure the wires from the batteries never come loose from their connections so that they can touch each other. This can cause a direct short across the batteries, wearing them out. Worse, it can potentially cause dangerous heat and even fire! Don't let any wires dangle!

When you're not playing with the R/C toy-turned-robot, remove its batteries and set them aside.

MOUNT THE BATTERY HOLDER

Secure the battery holder to the switch plate to keep the batteries from flopping around:

1 Peel off the protective covering from one side of a 1" x 1" square of double-sided foam tape.

2 Apply the tape to the underside of the battery holder.

3 Peel off the covering from the other side of the tape and secure the holder to the lower end of the switch plate.

TEST THE R/C CAR USING YOUR HOMEBREW SWITCH

Let's try out the robot control switch you've just constructed:

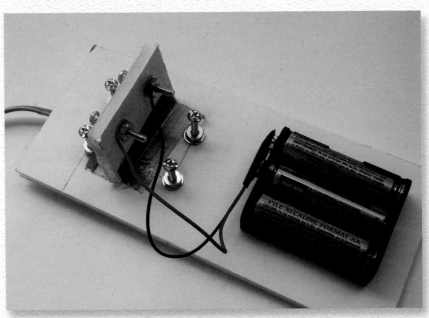

Go forward*:
touch the switch
to these terminals

Go backward*:
touch the switch
to these terminals

*Forward and back
depend on the wiring
of your R/C.

1 Place the switch in its "neutral" position — that is, so that none of the screws touch one another.

2 Insert three fresh alkaline batteries into the battery holder.

3 Place the R/C toy on top of some paperback books, so that the wheels don't touch the ground.

4 Toggle the switch forward and back — the drive wheels on the toy should spin one direction, then the other.

Oops — nothing happened? Try these fixes:

» **Be sure the batteries are fresh.** Use only new, fresh alkaline batteries.

» **Check that none of the wires have come loose.** Remake any bad connection.

» **As needed, peel off the tape covering the connection between the telephone line cord and the motor wires in the R/C toy.** Be sure these haven't come loose.

With testing complete, put the R/C toy on the ground and flip the switch to make it go.

If the vehicle goes backward when you push the switch forward, you can simply turn the entire switch base around so that the switch is upside down; or you can reverse the telephone cord wires that attach to the bottom of the switch plate.

SUBSTITUTING WITH READYMADE SWITCHES

Making your own switch from scratch is a great way to learn the basics of motor control, not to mention how switches work. But homespun switches are bulky and cumbersome. So let's improve the robot builder's platform by substituting your DIY contraption with two commercially made toggle switches.

EXTRA PARTS YOU NEED

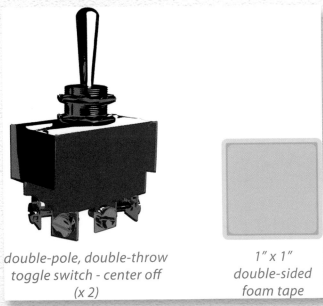

double-pole, double-throw toggle switch - center off (x 2)

1" x 1" double-sided foam tape

You need two DPDT (double-pole, double-throw) toggle switches: one for the drive motor, and one for the steering motor. Get the heavy-duty kind with screw terminals so you don't have to solder anything.

You need the type with a center-off position (the spring-loaded kind that returns to the center-off position when you let go of the switch is the best). With center-off, the switch has three positions:

» On

» Off

» On

The motor turns in either of the *on* positions.

Heavy duty DPDT toggle switches can be expensive if purchased at a local home improvement store. Save some money and get them online from an electronics outfit. See "Finding the Stuff to Build Your Robots," at the back of this book, for suggestions. I bought the ones used in the prototype for under $4 each.

WIRE THE SWITCHES

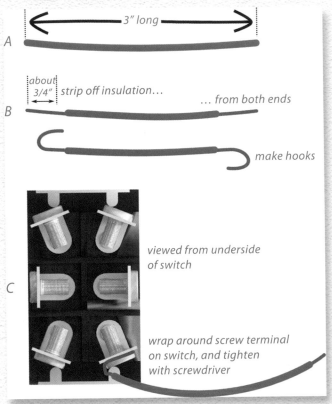

A

← 3" long →

B

about 3/4" strip off insulation...

... from both ends

make hooks

C

viewed from underside of switch

wrap around screw terminal on switch, and tighten with screwdriver

Like the homebrew version, the switches are wired to make an H-bridge circuit. This allows you to control the direction of the drive and steering motors.

Take one switch and

1 Create the crisscross of the H-bridge circuit by cutting two lengths of 3" solid core wire.

2 Strip off about 3/4" of insulation from either end of the wires.

3 Loosen the four outermost screws of the switch and, in a crisscross fashion, attach the wires to these terminals.

4 Make little hooks in the wires to wrap them around the screw posts. Tighten the screws.

Not all DPDT switches are wired the same internally (although such switches tend to be rare). Check with any specification sheet that comes with the switch to make sure that the two center posts on the switch are the common connections. The four outer connections should be the outputs of the switch.

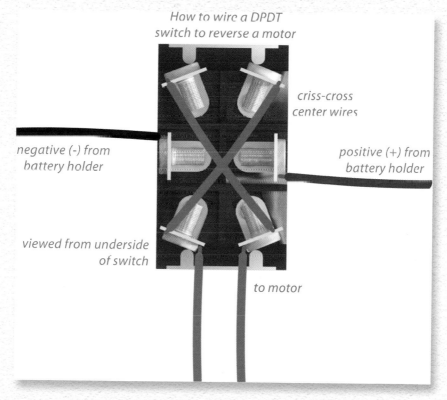

How to wire a DPDT switch to reverse a motor

criss-cross center wires

negative (-) from battery holder

positive (+) from battery holder

viewed from underside of switch

to motor

5 Connect the red wire from the battery holder to one of the center terminals of the switch. Don't tighten the screw just yet.

6 Connect the black wire from the battery holder to the other center terminal. Don't tighten.

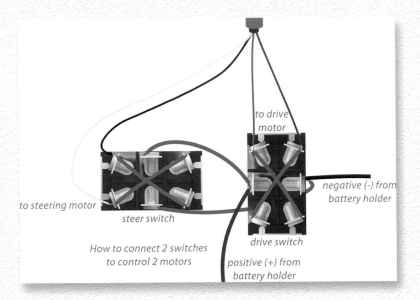

to drive motor

negative (-) from battery holder

to steering motor

steer switch

How to connect 2 switches to control 2 motors

drive switch

positive (+) from battery holder

7 Cut two lengths of 6" solid wire and remove about 3/4" of insulation on both ends.

8 Attach these two wires to the center terminals you used in Steps 6 and 7. Okay, now tighten the screws.

That takes care of the drive motor. You now need to wire up the steering motor:

1 Following the steps in the section "Attach the Wires to the R/C Car Motor," connect the remaining two wires from the telephone line cord to the steering motor in your R/C vehicle.

Be sure the bare wire ends don't touch each other. Wrap the sliced wires in electrical tape to both insulate and protect them.

2 Using the second switch, repeat Steps 1 through 4 from the preceding list.

3 Connect the two 6" lengths of wire from the first switch to the center terminals of this switch.

4 **For each switch: Pick one of the ends — it doesn't matter which one. Loosen the screw terminals on this end, and attach the motor wires from the telephone line cord. Tighten the screws.**

Be sure the wire colors match up to the motors they connect to on your R/C car. Otherwise, the motors will not run.

You may now mount the switches and battery holder to a new switch plate.

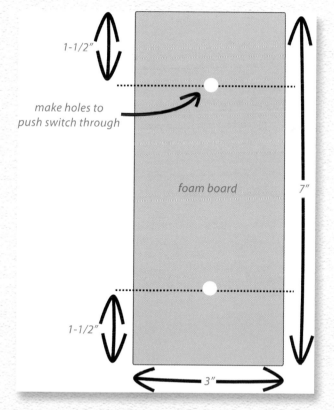

1 **Cut a piece of 3" x 7" foam board.**

2 **About 1" from either end, use a screwdriver to poke a hole through the board.**

3 Enlarge the hole with a pen or pencil. Make it big enough so that you can push the stem of the switches all the way through.

4 Remove the retaining nut from both switches, and insert the switch through the bottom of the foam board. Twist the retaining nut back onto the switch.

5 Attach the battery holder following the steps in the section, "Mount the Battery Holder."

RUN THE R/C CAR THROUGH ITS PACES

As you did with the homebrew switch, test your creation by placing both switches in the *off* position. Then,

1 Insert fresh alkaline batteries into the battery holder.

2 Place the R/C toy on top of some paperback books so that the wheels don't touch the ground.

3 Toggle both switches forward and back. The drive and steering motors should activate.

Orient the two switches to reflect their respective jobs: (a) The drive motor switch should toggle up and down; and (b) The steering motor switch should toggle right and left.

GOING FURTHER

We've only just scratched the surface of what you can do with your new robot experimenter's platform. Several bonus projects are provided online at www.robotpalace.com/byob/.

Some projects may require help from an adult. See the bonus project plans for details.

Here are some ideas you might try:

» **Remove the hardwired switches and use a completely electronic circuit to control your R/C vehicle.** Make it move and turn by shining a bright flashlight at it.

» **Hook up your R/C vehicle to an inexpensive Arduino microcontroller board (about $25).** Download simple programs to the Arduino to operate the motors and to respond to sensor input.

» **Have your friends hack their own radio-controlled toy, and hold competitions.** Download a print-and-cut template for the foam board pieces at www.dummies.com/go/buildingyourownrobots.

AUTHOR NOTES

FINDING THE STUFF TO BUILD YOUR ROBOTS

I DON'T KNOW ABOUT YOU, BUT I THINK ONE OF THE MOST ENJOYABLE ASPECTS OF CONSTRUCTING ROBOTS IS FINDING THE PARTS TO MAKE THEM!

You should always start your stuff-search by scavenging through your own closet or garage. See if you already have the parts you need. If not, you can then turn to the local and online resources.

I can't help you find things on some dusty shelf in your attic, but here's a short list I've prepared with some well-respected retailers for your robo-making hobby.

An asterisk (*) denotes a store I used for parts and materials in the writing of this book.

DISCOUNT GENERAL MERCHANDISE, SUPPLIES, AND TOOLS

Items of interest: inexpensive tools and building materials (including electrical tape and foam board), battery-operated toothbrushes, friction-drive toy cars.

99 Cents Only* (www.99only.com)

Big Lots (www.biglots.com)

Dollar General (www.dollargeneral.com)

Dollar Tree* (www.dollartree.com)

These stores are both online and local — however, physical stores may be restricted by state, and online sites may not sell directly to consumers.

Be sure also to check out independent dollar and discount stores in your area.

ELECTRICAL SUPPLIES

Items of interest: 22 gauge wire (stranded and solid), 1.5-to-3 volt toy motors, double-pole, double-throw toggle switches (with screw terminals), wire cutting/stripping tools, electrical tape, battery holders, rechargeable batteries and rechargers.

All Electronics* (www.allelectronics.com)

BG Micro* (www.bgmicro.com)

Jameco (www.jameco.com)

Marlin P. Jones Assoc. (www.mpja.com)

Pololu (www.pololu.com) (for motors, verify they are rated 3V)

Radio Shack (www.radioshack.com) (local stores in some areas)

TOYS FOR DISASSEMBLY

Items of interest: under-$25 full-function radio-controlled vehicles and friction-drive toy cars.

Amazon (www.amazon.com) (department: Toys, Kids & Baby)

K-Mart (www.kmart.com) (department: Toys)

Toys-R-Us (www.toysrus.com)

Wal-Mart* (www.walmart.com) (department: Toys & Video Games)

TOOLS AND ELECTRICAL SUPPLY

Items of interest: general tools (screwdrivers, hot melt glue gun, and so on), wire cutting/stripping tools, electrical tape, duct tape, rubber tubing, metal fasteners.

Harbor Freight (www.harborfreight.com)

Home Depot* (www.homedepot.com)

Lowe's (www.lowes.com)

These stores are both online and local. Physical stores may be restricted by state.

Be sure to check out local hardware and home improvement stores, many of which have a deeper selection of items.

ROBOT-MAKING KITS AND PARTS

Items of interest: readymade kits for building robots, motors, learning-to-solder kits, and other component parts.

Adafruit (www.adafruit.com)

Fry's (www.frys.com) (stores in some states)

Micro Center (www.microcenter.com) (stores in some states)

Parallax (www.parallax.com)

Pololu (www.pololu.com)

Robot Shop (www.robotshop.com) (ships from US, Canada, Europe)

Scientifics Online (www.scientificsonline.com)

Solarbotics (www.solarbotics.com)

Sparkfun (www.sparkfun.com)

ROBOTICS INFORMATION, BUILDING PLANS, AND BLOGS

Items of interest: robotics news, reviews of robot kits, and robot construction plans and ideas.

Hackaday (http://hackaday.com)

Instructables (www.instructables.com)

Makezine Blog (http://makezine.com/blog)

Robot Grrl (http://robotgrrl.com/blog)

Robot Shop Blog (www.robotshop.com/blog)

Robot Palace Blog (www.robotpalace.com/byob)

Trossen Robotics Blog (http://blog.trossenrobotics.com)

SELECTED INTERNATIONAL SELLERS

Although most of the online sources here ship internationally, if you're not in North America, you may prefer buying from someone more local to help keep down the costs of shipping. Here are a few selected international sellers of kits, electrical supplies and tools, toys, and other merchandise you'll find helpful in your robot-building.

Altronics (www.altronics.com.au) (Australia)

Jaycar (www.jaycar.com.au) (Australia)

Maplin (www.maplin.co.uk) (UK)

Pimoroni (http://pimoroni.com) (UK)

Robot Shop (www.robotshop.com) (Canada, EU)

Tesco (www.tesco.com) (UK)

GLOSSARY

Stuck on what a particular word means, and how it relates to the robot you're building right now? Here are some definitions you'll want to know.

battery: A self-contained module used to power your robot. Batteries come in two broad types; non-rechargeable (dispose when depleted) and rechargeable (recharge to full capacity again and again). Alkaline batteries are an example of the non-rechargeable kind; nickel-metal hydride batteries are an example of rechargeable.

brushbot: A popular type of robot that uses a small brush, vibrating motor, and battery. The vibration of the motor causes the bristles of the brush to skate across a smooth surface.

car-type steering: A method of steering a robot similar to that of a car: Drive wheels in the rear make it go forward and back, and turning wheels in the front make it steer.

circuit: A complete electrical system. In robotics, a circuit typically comprises a power source, wiring, motors, switches, and other components for activating and controlling the robot.

differential steering: A method of steering with just two wheels, one on each side, to both steer and move the robot forward and back.

double-pole, double-throw (DPDT):   A type of switch that contains multiple contact points, often used in robotics for controlling the direction of a motor. Other switch types include single-pole, single-throw (SPST) and single-pole, double-throw (SPDT).

friction drive: A type of toy that uses a heavy wheel (called the flywheel) so that when you push it along the floor, the momentum from the heavy spinning wheel keeps it moving for longer that it might otherwise go.

foam board: A common type of art material used in constructing robots. It consists of an inner core of squishy Styrofoam (or similar material) with heavy paper glued to the top and bottom.

H-bridge: A type of electronic circuit that allows the polarity of a battery to be reversed. This allows for motors to turn in either direction.

hot melt glue: A type of glue that is applied through a gunlike applicator tool. The tool heats up the glue, which is in the form of a stick, and deposits it on the surfaces you want to bond.

insulation: For wiring, a plastic covering that protects the wires inside and prevents them from touching other parts of the robot that they shouldn't.

motor: An electrical component that, when power is applied (as from a battery), causes a shaft to rotate, usually at high speeds. Motors are commonly used in the construction of robots.

polarity: In batteries, denotes the two connecting terminals on the cell, either positive (+) or negative (–).

radio-controlled (R/C):   A method of operating a toy or robot using radio signals.

robot: Technically, a machine that combines autonomous (works on its own) functions, with various sensors (seeing, hearing, touching) so it can interact with its environment. In practical use, what counts as a *robot* encompasses a much wider field, such as human-controlled motorized vehicles for "robot combat" competitions.

stranded wire: Wire that is composed of many smaller strands, bundled together. This is as opposed to solid wire, which has just one large strand.

subsystem: A separate component part that, when combined with others, makes a complete robot.

switch: A common electrical component used for controlling the power in a circuit.

vibrating motor: A type of motor that has an off-centered weight attached to its shaft. When the shaft turns, the weight causes an unbalance and makes the entire motor shake.

volt: A basic unit of measurement in electronics that denotes "electric potential," a kind of energy produced by batteries, solar cells, and similar devices. Example: Many consumer batteries produce 1.5 volts.

wire gauge: A system of identifying the diameter of a wire. The smaller the number, the larger the wire. For home-based robotics, 22 gauge wire is appropriate.

ABOUT THE AUTHOR

Gordon McComb is the author of more than 65 books. His passion is building robots and letting them run amok in the house.

AUTHOR'S ACKNOWLEDGMENTS

My humble gratitude to Lane, Jennifer, Mercedes, and Marshall for their ideas and suggestions. Special thanks to Firen and Teemo, for being such great photography models!

PUBLISHER'S ACKNOWLEDGMENTS

Senior Acquisitions Editor:
Amy Fandrei

Production Editor:
Tamilmani Varadharaj

Project Editor: Christopher Morris

Copy Editor: Christopher Morris

Editorial Assistant: Serena Novosel

Senior Editorial Assistant:
Cherie Case

Technical Reviewer: Connor Morris